TEACHING THE CRITICAL
VOCABULARY
OF THE COMMON CORE

MARILEE SPRENGER

TEACHING THE CRITICAL

VOCABULARY

OF THE COMMON CORE

55 WORDS THAT MAKE OR BREAK STUDENT UNDERSTANDING

Alexandria, Virginia USA

1703 N. Beauregard St. • Alexandria, VA 22311-1714 USA
Phone: 800-933-2723 or 703-578-9600 • Fax: 703-575-5400
Website: www.ascd.org • E-mail: member@ascd.org
Author guidelines: www.ascd.org/write

Gene R. Carter, *Executive Director;* Ed Milliken, *Interim Chief Program Development Officer;* Richard Papale, *Publisher;* Stefani Roth, *Acquisitions Editor;* Julie Houtz, *Director, Book Editing & Production;* Deborah Siegel, *Editor;* Sima Nasr, *Senior Graphic Designer;* Mike Kalyan, *Production Manager;* Cynthia Stock, *Typesetter;* Andrea Wilson, *Production Specialist*

PAPERBACK ISBN: 978-1-4166-1571-2   ASCD product # 113040   n6/13
Also available as an e-book (see Books in Print for the ISBNs).

Quantity discounts: 10–49 copies, 10%; 50+ copies, 15%; for 1,000 or more copies, call 800-933-2723, ext. 5634, or 703-575-5634. For desk copies: www.ascd.org/deskcopy

Library of Congress Cataloging-in-Publication Data

Sprenger, Marilee, 1949–
  Teaching the critical vocabulary of the common core : 55 words that make or break student understanding / Marilee Sprenger.
     pages cm
  Includes bibliographical references and index.
  ISBN 978-1-4166-1571-2 (pbk. : alk. paper) 1. Vocabulary—Study and teaching—United States.
2. Education—Standards—United States. I. Title.
  LB1574.5.S725 2013
  372.44—dc23
                                                                    2013007228

22 21 20 19 18 17 16 15   3 4 5 6 7 8 9 10 11 12

Dedication

This book is dedicated to all teachers who work hard every day to help students increase their background knowledge and their success in school and life by building their vocabularies. I hope this helps. This is also for my students who needed more help than I knew how to give them. I wish I had a second chance. I am still learning.

TEACHING THE CRITICAL

VOCABULARY
OF THE COMMON CORE

Acknowledgments

I want to thank the teachers and students who let me "quiz" them on the critical vocabulary words in this book. They gave me the inspiration and vision to write something that would help with the Common Core State Standards. To my own students I owe a debt of gratitude, especially those who had trouble with vocabulary and made me work harder to come up with ideas that would help them.

Special thanks to Genny Ostertag, Stefani Roth, and the ASCD book acquisitions team who feel this work is important for educators to have in their hands as soon as possible. I am grateful for the confidence and encouragement. Deborah Siegel, associate editor, has been a champion in trying to see my vision and make the information in this book easy to access and use.

Of course, I must acknowledge my husband, Scott, who puts up with the late hours and the missed dinners while I am working on a project. The entire family is supportive: my two children, Josh and Marnie, are always in the back of my mind as I write for very different learners. Amy, my daughter-in-law, is a new author, and her diligence keeps me motivated. Jack, Emmie, and Maeven, my grandchildren, are inspirational as I watch their vocabularies increase each day.

Introduction

With the adoption of the Common Core State Standards (CCSS) by most states, there has been a sense of urgency for some educators and a sense of impending doom for others. As the tension grows for all, I looked for a place to start making the brain what I call "core compatible." Neuroscience research has provided us with information that has been translated into classroom practice. We now know how to help most students.

For the past several years, I have been sharing the research that suggests that standardized tests are based on the vocabulary of the standards. We discuss the 85 percent conclusion (the idea that 85 percent of test scores are based on how well students know the vocabulary of the standards) that Marzano (Tileston, 2011) and others have researched. The teachers were much like my students, nodding that they knew this information and confirming that they were teaching the vocabulary. As a result, I assumed that they were using this exciting bit of knowledge to jumpstart their students to success. But why were test scores dismal at so many schools? Just as I would believe those nods and yeses from the kids, I believed the teachers as well. And the truth is, we do teach much of the vocabulary, but we do not teach it well enough. After all, who does not ask students to analyze, compare, or summarize? As I think about my own classrooms, I realize that with some students who were less familiar with terms like these, I would break them down for them as I cruised the room to help when I saw confusion on their faces. Instead of reiterating that we were working on compare and contrast, I would say, "Just write down what is the same and what is different." So, they knew what I wanted them to do, but the word itself, which they would run into on assessments, was often lost.

I started doing some research of my own. Whenever I was in a classroom during the past year, I asked students simple questions like, "Can you describe what is in this picture?" "Contrast those ratios." "Analyze the poem." From kindergartener Jack to 6th grader Liza, I got little response. Jack did understand *compare* when I asked, "Can you compare your lunch with Emily's?" At the next table, however, Sam could not. When I headed to the high schools, I thought it would be different. I was disappointed to discover that many of the students had difficulty with the words. Of course, those from low-income families and English language learners had the most trouble. What if some of the difficulty our schools have with raising student achievement is as simple as teaching and reinforcing these words?

I wondered about my own students. Had I prepared them for their tests? Did I teach them the right words? I thought I had. But how did I teach them? Did the learning stick? I remember the rush to get things covered. Was I really taking into consideration the memory research? *Was I teaching it quick but not making it stick?*

As we transition to the Common Core standards, we have the opportunity to truly prepare our students for their futures. We must do everything we can to ensure their success. This book is intended to give everyone the jumpstart they need. The words in this book are not uncommon, but for one reason or another, they have not entered most of our students' long-term memories nor have they been rehearsed to a point where they are automatically recognized, defined, and acted upon.

I call the words in this book "critical." The definitions of *critical* include indispensable, essential, urgently needed, absolutely necessary, decisive, momentous, pressing, serious, vital, urgent, all-important, pivotal, high-priority, now or never. **The definitions of the word *critical* tell us the story.**

As we head into the regular use of the Common Core standards, it is *essential* that our students master these words. It will be *absolutely necessary* for them to automatically know the definitions without using precious working memory. If they must search their brains to understand what the questions on the assessment are asking of them, they are wasting precious time and brain space needed to analyze their readings and answer the questions. These words should be the first group of Tier 2 words to tackle. *Critical* also is defined as "now or never." The time is now to transition to the CCSS. The students who are comfortable with these words will be the most successful in mastering the standards. These words will be indispensable on assessments and in life.

Teaching these words is urgent in order to assist students in understanding what is expected of them as they tackle complex texts, learn to read more closely, add to their vocabularies, improve speaking and listening skills, and become well-rounded learners and members of society.

Chapter 1 addresses research on vocabulary. It is necessary to know how students acquire words and their meanings. Research offers steps that can be followed for most vocabulary words. The critical words will require more from teachers and students, but this is valuable background knowledge.

Chapter 2 explains how memory works. The brain has memory systems and pathways that work in different ways. The procedural nonmotor system is the memory system that works for placing these words and definitions in the brain so they are instantly accessible.

Chapter 3 describes the critical verbs. The association of these verbs with the CCSS helps motivate us to teach these important words. Various strategies such as jingles, 2-D and 3-D graphic organizers, computer games, and movement activities along with the research on these and other strategies are presented. Then the fun begins with pages devoted to each verb along with suggested activities to help all students learn and remember them.

The critical nouns are introduced in Chapter 4. Following some general information for remembering the types of ideas and concepts that words represent, the nouns themselves will be introduced one by one with activities to help you create lessons for them.

Chapter 5 provides a few more words that are important for some grade levels but are not nouns or verbs.

Chapter 6 includes information about the Common Core vocabulary standards.

Chapter 7 offers basic ideas on keeping these words alive in the minds of our students. Words of the week, usage across content areas, and using these words on classroom assessments and in classroom conversations are a few of the fundamental strategies mentioned.

The appendix provides templates for many of the strategies used throughout the book.

Once these words are embedded in our students' long-term memories, they will become part of our common conversations as we teach to the CCSS.

How to Use This Book

If you are like me, you may need to read this book from beginning to end. I suggest you read the first three chapters and dive into those verbs! Once you have those critical words going, read Chapter 4 and decide if you need to teach all of the critical nouns or just a few.

There are some strategies repeated and others only described once. They are all useful strategies, and don't think that the ones that are in a particular word's section are all you should use for that word. I tried to offer as many different strategies as I could, but you have your own toolbox to use.

If you consider these words valuable for your students and I have offered you some ideas on how to teach them, then I will have accomplished my goal.

CHAPTER 1

What Does the Research Say About Vocabulary?

One of the key indicators of students' success in school, on standardized tests, and indeed, in life, is their vocabulary. The reason for this is simply that the knowledge anyone has about a topic is based on the vocabulary of that information (Marzano & Pickering, 2005). For instance, as you read the following sentence, see if you are able to determine what is being discussed.

A duct-less split can produce the exact amount of energy needed to temper an envelope.

When I first read this sentence, my mind started to try to make connections to envelopes and wondered if tempering had something to do with getting or keeping the glue on the flap. If you are an engineer, you probably know that the sentence above refers to equipment and its capability of cooling a room. As with any topic, the more you know about heating and cooling, the easier it is to learn and understand information about it.

There are a variety of factors that affect student achievement, including the effectiveness of the teacher, the student's own personal interest in the content matter, and the amount of information students already possess about the content. "Prior knowledge" is a term with which most educators are familiar. In neuroscience terms, we are talking about long-term memory. And, yes, prior knowledge, also known as background knowledge, consists of networks in the brain that have been placed in permanent memory. In this chapter we will consider how students obtain knowledge about subject matter and how vocabulary supports this knowledge.

The Background on Background Knowledge

According to Marzano (2004), background knowledge is acquired through the interaction of two factors: the ability of the student to process and store information (which will be covered in Chapter 2), and the regularity with which a student has academically oriented experiences. Professional educators know that the amount of background knowledge our students have may rely a great deal on their cultural differences and their economic status (Tileston & Darling, 2008).

Not only does background knowledge grow in the brains of our students through their experiences, but the vocabulary words that are stored as a result of such experiences provide avenues to comprehend the curriculum from the text, as well as lecture and discussion. We can look at the work of Piaget (1970), who concluded that we organize information in our brains in the form of a schema, a representation of concepts, ideas, and actions that are related.

Schemata (the plural of *schema*) are formed in our brains through repeated and varied experiences related to a topic. As a neuroeducator, one who teaches students and teachers based on current brain research, I like to refer to schemata as those networks in the brain that we form, store, re-form, and restore through our interactions in the world through both experience and environment. It is the brain's ability to change known as neuroplasticity that allows us to learn and form lasting memories. (Doidge, 2007). Yet, as new evidence presents itself, the brain can change to accommodate the new information.

Often long-term memory is compared to files in our brains. Just as you store files on your computer or tablet, the brain stores information in ways that allow it to retrieve concepts, ideas, and actions in an orderly and expeditious manner. Consider, if you will, the file you have stored for "school."

As an educator, you may have stored in that file what you liked or loved about school that brought you to the classroom and perhaps beyond. In that file you may also have memories of your own school days, beginning with preschool and going through the university degrees you may have. Certain teachers who are role models for you are stored in this file, as are teachers you would not want to emulate. If you have been in education for a while, there are many "buzzwords" that have been used throughout the years that were considered best practices in teaching. Today you have probably added terms like *differentiation, Response-to-Intervention,* and *Common Core State Standards.* All of this, and much more, refers to your background knowledge of "school."

All of our students have a school file (or schema) in their brains as well. Their files are likely very unique to their experiences with schools and teachers, their cultures, their parents views of education, and their personal success in school.

It is no easy task to build background knowledge in students who enter our classrooms with few academic experiences from other classrooms or from real-world involvement. Background knowledge is a reflection of who they are; it is the lens through which they see the world. Those students from low-income families see school in a different light. School may be a place to be safe when home is not. School may be inconsequential to those who believe their "street smarts" will get them farther in life than school smarts. School may feel dangerous to some students whose parents identify school as a place where they felt stupid or unappreciated. Many students from impoverished backgrounds enter school with little knowledge of a world outside the streets where they live. If their poverty was pervasive throughout their short lives, factors such as lack of nutrition or exposure to toxins may have stunted the growth of their brains, which affects their cognitive abilities (Perry, 2001).

According to educational research by Hart and Risley (1995), children enter school with "meaningful differences." The differences that did not appear to be meaningful were things like race, ethnicity, birth order, or gender. What made a big difference among students was economics. In their book, *Meaningful Differences in the Everyday Experiences of Young American*

Children (1995), Hart and Risley state, "by age 3 the children in professional families would have heard more than 30 million words, the children in working class families 20 million, and the children in welfare families 10 million" (p. 132). Interestingly, although the number of words spoken was different, the topics and the style of speech were similar. The parents who spoke to their children more began to ask questions, vary their vocabulary, and in general offered the kids a rich language experience. In addition to counting the number of words that were spoken to the children, Hart and Risley also examined the types of reinforcement the children received. The number of affirmative statements as opposed to prohibitory statements was tallied for each socioeconomic group. The professional parents offered affirmative feedback much more often (every other minute) than the other groups. The welfare parents gave their children more than twice as many prohibitions as the professional parents. Some children in professional families heard 450 different words and 210 questions in the three hours the parent spoke most. Another child from a low-income family heard fewer than 200 different words and 38 questions in that same amount of time. The results of the study lead all to believe that the single-most important component of child care is the amount of talking occurring between child and caregiver.

Consider these facts:

- Vocabulary is a strong indicator of student success (Baker, Simmons, & Kame'enui, 1997).
- The number of words students learn varies greatly:

  2 vs. 8 words per **day**
  750 vs. 3,000 per **year**

- Printed school English, as represented by materials in grades 3 to 9, contains 88,533 distinct word families (Nagy & Anderson, 1984).
- 88,533 word families result in total volumes of nearly 500,000 graphically distinct word types, including proper names. Roughly half of 500,000 words occur once or less in a billion words of text (Nagy & Anderson, 1984).

- In grades 3 through 12, an average student is likely to learn approximately 3,000 new vocabulary words each year, if he or she reads between 500,000 and a million running words of text a school year (Nagy & Anderson, 1984).
- Between grades 1 and 3, it is expected that economically disadvantaged students' vocabularies increase by about 3,000 words per year, while middle-class students' vocabularies increase by about 5,000 words per year.
- Children's vocabulary size approximately doubles between grades 3 and 7.

More recent research added pertinent information to vocabulary development. Dr. Catherine Tamis-LeMonda of New York University and Dr. Marc Borstein of the National Institutes of Health approached the topic of vocabulary development in a different way. They compared maternal responsiveness in children who all came from professional families, with interesting results. (Remember that the children from professional families heard 30 million words by age 3.) The study found that the average child spoke his or her first words by 13 months and by 18 months had a vocabulary of about 50 words. Mothers who were considered high responders—that is, they responded to their child's speech quickly and often—had children who were clearly 6 months ahead of the children whose mothers were low responders. These toddlers spoke their first words at 10 months and had high vocabularies and the ability to speak in short sentences by 14 months (Bronson & Merryman, 2009).

Poverty, the Brain, and Vocabulary

Students from low-income families are part of the at-risk population who have heard fewer words and may have brains that are not as cognitively efficient for some of the work ahead of them in school and in life. Research supports the need for these students to have some extra resources. The remarkable ability of the brain to change has been seen in students with many different kinds of deficits. Poverty can cause physical differences in the brain as well as behavioral differences (Jensen, 2009). According to Harris (2006), three areas drive school behavior:

1. **A desire for reliable relationships.** Much research looks at the teacher-student relationship as a driving force for motivation, socialization, and academic performance.

2. **A desire for social acceptance by peers.** In order for students to seek academic achievement, it must be socially acceptable to achieve it. Your school must create a culture that supports and encourages good academic behavior.

3. **A desire for social status.** Students want to feel special. The emotional brain contains an affective filter that will allow information to go to higher levels of thinking under the right conditions. Negative feelings, lack of social status, and low peer acceptance will keep the brain focused on these and prevent cognitive function.

How Are the Brains of Poor Kids Different?

Several areas of the brain are different in low-income and middle-income students. Using the work of Farah, Noble, and Hurt (2005), we can examine five systems that are responsible for overall school functioning:

- The executive system, which engages the prefrontal cortex of the brain. This structure is crucial to working memory, future planning, delaying gratification, and decision making.
- The language system, which involves the temporal and frontal lobes of the left hemisphere. This system is our reading system and contains the structures that allow students to decode, pronounce, and comprehend.
- The memory system, which allows students to process semantic learning (text, lecture, pictures, etc.) and then store it. This system is responsible for one-trial learning and the ability to retain a representation of a stimulus after a single exposure to it. Our emotional center and our memory center are next to each other, which explains why emotions influence our memories.

- The cognitive system, which includes our visual spatial abilities and our problem-solving capabilities of the parietal lobe. This system is vital to sequencing, organizing, and visualizing.
- The visual cognitive system, which allows students to recognize patterns, remember images, and abstract information.

The results of testing these systems in several studies remained fairly constant. The lower the socioeconomic status, the more difficulty the students had performing tasks involving these systems. Most noticeable were the memory system issues and the language system issues. The group tested middle school students and primary students with the same results. These issues affect not only school performance, but life performance as well.

As researchers continue to study the effects of poverty on academic performance, they know there are a myriad of possible causes of these issues. It is not the purpose of this book to delve into those causes. I will suggest that most research examines prenatal toxins, maternal stress, lack of proper nutrition, living in toxic areas, maternal education, and the amount of language and literacy in the home.

Improving the Systems

Because the brain is malleable and these systems can change, researchers have made several suggestions to improve the brain systems of low-SES children.

- Gazzaniga, Asbury, and Rich (2008) suggest the arts can improve cognitive skills, processing, attention, and sequencing.
- Pereira and colleagues (2007) suggest physical activity as an avenue to produce new brain cells, which has been associated with increasing learning and memory.
- Computer instruction in which students identify, count, and remember objects by holding them in working memory can increase working memory within a matter of weeks, according to Klingberg and colleagues (2005).
- Training in music can improve the brain's operating systems as it enhances focused attention, which will assist in memory (Jonides, 2008).

The arts, movement, computer use, and music are some of the strategies that will be helpful in teaching all of our students the vocabulary of the standards. Understanding and being aware of some of the challenges that our at-risk students face will help us to focus our vocabulary teaching in a way that will improve the minds and memories of our students.

The Three Tiers

In 1985, Beck and McKeown suggested that every literate person has a vocabulary consisting of three levels (Beck, McKeown, & Kucan, 2002). Tier 1 words consist of basic words. These words usually do not have multiple meanings and do not require explicit instruction. Sight words, nouns, verbs, adjectives, and early reading words occur at this level. Examples of Tier 1 words are *book, girl, sad, clock, baby, dog,* and *orange.* There are about 8,000 word families in English included in Tier 1. Tier 2 contains high-frequency words that occur across a variety of domains. These words play a large role in the vocabulary of mature language users. As a result, Tier 2 words may have a large impact in the everyday functioning of language. Because of their lack of redundancy in oral language, Tier 2 words present challenges to students who primarily meet them in print. Tier 2 words consist of such words as *coincidence, masterpiece, absurd, industrious,* and *benevolent.* Because Tier 2 words play an important role in direct instruction, there are certain characteristics that these words have:

- Usually have multiple meanings
- Used in a variety of subject areas
- Necessary for reading comprehension
- Characteristic of a mature language user
- Descriptive words that add detail

Tier 3 consists of words whose practical use and frequency is low. These words are domain-specific and are used for brief periods of time when we are studying particular content. Tier 3 words are central to building knowledge and conceptual understanding within the various academic domains and should be integral to instruction of content. Medical, legal, biology and mathematics terms are all examples of these words. Although useful while covering specific topics, these are too specific to be included in the most useful tier for vocabulary building, Tier 2.

The CCSS stress that learning and using vocabulary is an essential component to college and career readiness, and references to it appear throughout the grade-level standards.

How do students add words to their mental lexicon? It begins with listening to the conversations in the early environment. Then vocabulary would be enhanced through listening to adults read aloud. Because stories contain vocabulary words not used in daily conversation, this is an excellent way to expand vocabulary. Students who come to our schools from a literacy-rich home are clearly in a better position to meet the CCSS. But the neuroplasticity of the brain teaches us that all students can learn, enhance their vocabulary, and change their brains (Sprenger, 2005).

The "How" of Teaching Vocabulary

In *Building Academic Vocabulary: Teacher's Manual* by Marzano and Pickering (2005), the following steps are recommended:

1. Begin with a story or explanation of the term. Modeling how you use the word in your life or in conversation may be helpful to students.
2. Have students put information into their own words. This process, which I call "recoding," is necessary to make sure students understand the word. This is a vital step in the memory process. Skipping this step can be disastrous as students may have a misconception that will be placed in long-term memory through incorrect rehearsals (Sprenger, 2005).
3. Ask students to draw a picture or a graphic representation of the word. According to Ruby Payne (2009), if students cannot draw it, they really don't know it.
4. Provide several engagements with the term and have students write them in a notebook. Research suggests that writing is good for the

brain and memory, so using those notebooks or some other platform for writing is important (Snowdon, 2001).

5. Informal rehearsals are just as important as formal ones. Engage students casually in conversation using the term. Putting them in pairs and letting them discuss their definitions is a good way to see if all students are storing the same information.

6. Play games with the words. Games are a brain-compatible strategy for reinforcing learning. Actively processing vocabulary words in multiple ways allows the brain to store information in multiple memory systems, thus making access to that information easier with multiple triggers or cues (Sprenger, 2010).

Why Worry About the Critical Words?

According to the neuroscientific research, my suggestion that it is "now or never" doesn't make much sense. But as a classroom teacher, I can tell you—and indeed, you can tell me—how important it is to get kids up to speed as quickly and efficiently as possible. Sure, anyone can learn the 55 or so words I consider critical to test taking, academics, and to life. But we should teach these words sooner rather than later to help our students increase test scores, build confidence, and put the words into daily use. Vocabulary has long been ignored or thought a burden in our classrooms. It is time to give it the time it deserves. Teaching vocabulary in fun and interesting ways will make learning new words something for all of us to look forward to.

CHAPTER 2

Processing and Storing Vocabulary

How often do you ask questions like this? "Does that make sense?" "Everybody got that?" "Are there any questions?" "Okay, did you write down that definition?" *Too often, we accept nods and smiles for understanding. This is often why by the time students leave our rooms—that is, walk out the door—they have forgotten what we think we have just taught them.*

We can look at the gradual release of responsibility model (Pearson & Gallagher, 1983) when we talk about processing vocabulary. The model is a four-part approach that begins with dependence and leads to independence in any area you are teaching. It always begins with the teacher. The GRR model, as it is often called, begins with teacher demonstration or modeling. In this phase, the control is in the hands of the teacher. The next step is guided by the teacher with student help or interaction. In step 3, the teacher offers some support, but most of the responsibility is on the student. Finally, the student is completely independent. Although the model looks like it is a simple four-step process, more time may be spent on different levels depending on the needs of the students. (See Figure 2.1.)

When we introduce new words, step 1 may take many modeling opportunities. Step 2 may consist of more interaction between teacher and

FIGURE 2.1
Gradual Release of Responsibility for Vocabulary

I DO IT	Discussing the vocabulary word; reading it in context.
WE DO IT TOGETHER	Looking up the dictionary definition and choosing a definition that sounds right for the context.
YOU DO IT TOGETHER	Students work in pairs or groups to come up with a definition in their own words.
YOU DO IT ALONE	Creating a mind map using the word as the focus.

students. Step 3 may involve creating and re-creating definitions, discussing why the definition works, and writing many sentences to help the word truly make sense to the students. Finally, step 4 shows only one example of the independent work. Learning the critical words will take many elaborate engagements in order to place the word in the memory system required for this type of long-term memory.

Many of these steps provide opportunities for formative assessment. Checking for understanding of the words and how they work in context is necessary to keep misinformation from becoming memories that have to be changed.

The goal of this book is to show you how to get these critical words, and other words as well, into long-term memory. It is helpful if you understand which memory system we will be using to do this. This chapter will very briefly give you some information on the brain and memory.

Two Kinds of Memory

Memory researchers like Squire and Kandel (2000) and Schacter (2001) teach us that memory is divided into declarative and nondeclarative memory. Some call these explicit memory and implicit memory.

Declarative, or explicit, memory is the kind of memory that you can and do talk about. It is your autobiographical memory, so this system is used when you give information about your life. It includes the people you know, the places you have been, and the experiences you have had.

Declarative memory can be divided into the episodic system and the semantic system. Episodic memory consists of those episodes in your life and can be very powerful in school. Students often remember what they learn after they first remember or visualize where they have learned it. Semantic memory consists of the memories that are made through the use of words. Lectures, textbooks, pictures that are discussed, video, and other media are included in this type of memory. As we get into learning the critical words, you will see how declarative memory plays a part in that process.

Nondeclarative is the type of memory I want you to understand as a valuable tool for teaching the critical words. Think of how you have taught reading, especially decoding and fluency, or how you teach multiplication tables. Although today's students can look up just about any information they need on the Internet, it is necessary for their brains to memorize some basics in order to understand larger ideas and concepts.

Nondeclarative memory is generally divided into two different categories: procedural memory that is motor based and procedural memory that is nonmotor. Riding a bike is a procedural motor skill; decoding words is a nonmotor procedural skill.

> *Aoccdrnig to rscheearch at Cmabrigde Uinervtisy, it deosn't mttaer in waht oredr the ltteers in a wrod are; the olny iprmoetnt tihng is taht the frist and lsat ltteer be at the rghit pclae. The rset can be a total mses and you can sitll raed it wouthit porbelm. Tihs is bcuseae the huamn mnid deos not raed ervey lteter by istlef, but the wrod as a wlohe. Amzanig, huh?*
>
> *PS: hwo'd you like to run this by your sepll ckehcer?*

Some version of the paragraph above has probably shown up in your email. Most of us read the paragraph with little effort. That is because we have thousands of words stored in our mental dictionary, the small brain structure in the left hemisphere called Wernicke's area. This lexicon has been built over the years and has the ability to store an unlimited amount of words.

Those of us who came from a strong literacy background from childhood have a larger stored vocabulary. Students who come from a background of little literacy and limited dialogue have a smaller lexicon. Therefore, the preceding paragraph of this chapter may be quite difficult for them. A dyslexic student may also have a limited mental dictionary and could struggle with words like *rscheearch*.

When students learn sight words and high-frequency words, they are committing the patterns in these words to memory. Every time we see the letters *t-h-e* we automatically know we are reading "the." *Automaticity* is the ability to do things without having to think about them at a conscious level. When we do something automatically, our mind isn't occupied with the small details of the task. This takes place because of our procedural memory system. Take a moment and think of the things you do at an automatic level. Driving a car comes to mind immediately. In fact, driving at that mindless level is a little scary. Have you ever gotten in your car on Saturday to go the grocery or the mall and found yourself driving the familiar path to school? Or arriving at a destination wondering how you got there or if you ran a red light? Fortunately the patterns that are stored in this procedural manner send an alarm whenever something seems amiss. You respond quickly if you look in your rear view mirror and see the red revolving light on the top of a police car.

Motor skills, such as riding a bike, are processed in several areas of the brain, including the prefrontal cortex and the cerebellum. In nonmotor procedural learning, such as decoding words, the brain area that appears to be most heavily involved is the visual cortex. As students rehearse their reading skills like committing the sight words to memory, those words are stored in many different ways, and initially they are stored pictorially. As the brain takes a snapshot of the words, it remembers the distinctions of the shapes and the lines, and a picture develops. With repeated practice, a long-term memory is formed. Remember that these changes do not involve understanding word meanings, only the ability to recognize the patterns more quickly. When students work on the meanings of words, more brain areas participate, including Wernicke's area.

The beauty of the automatic system in our brains is its ability to free up working memory. Working memory is the temporary system we use to get things done. You are using working memory as you read the words on this page. Your brain takes the information from the page, adds any prior knowledge you have of the topic, and gives you the space to comprehend what you are reading. Becoming a fluent reader necessitates the ability to use the automatic system. Riding a bike, brushing your teeth, adding low numbers, multiplying, and singing songs fall into the category of automatic memory.

All of this information leads us to the fact that many of our students, especially those from less advantaged backgrounds, those who are ELL students, and some with learning disabilities, have a more limited vocabulary and have not developed their automatic systems to the level necessary for our purposes.

The Bottom Line

To be successful with the CCSS, students need a smooth running automatic memory system to process and store the academic vocabulary of the standards.

Michael sits quietly at his seat, staring at the paper before him. His pencil is clenched in his hand. His eyes dart across the words on the page. He doesn't understand what is expected of him. As a result, he is embarrassed and a little panicky. This is a state test, and Michael knows he is not allowed to speak to anyone nearby. His feelings are troubling and he continues to look down at his paper and then down at his lap. As the minutes tick by on the clock, he feels more and more hopeless.

Mrs. Murphy observes the students as she sits at her desk. Occasionally, she cruises the room very quietly as to not disturb the students who appear to be working diligently. She sees Michael put his No. 2 pencil down. This does not bode well for Michael's test score. When time is up, Mrs. Murphy asks all students to put their pencils down and collects the test booklets and answer sheets in the appropriate manner.

At this point Mrs. Murphy approaches Michael.

"It looked like you were having some problems with the test, Michael. Did you have trouble reading the text selections?"

Still looking down, "No, ma'am."

"Then why weren't you answering the questions?"

"I didn't know what they wanted me to say."

"So, you understood the readings, but you didn't understand the question?"

"No, ma'am. I didn't know what that word meant, analyze.*"*

"But, Michael, we have gone over the definition of that word. You have done some activities in which you had to analyze how two articles addressed the same idea or theme. Do you remember that?"

"No, ma'am." Michael continues to look down, now at the floor. Mrs. Murphy looks concerned and gets on with the class.

I want to point out two things in this scenario. First, according to Michael, he read and understood the texts he had to read to answer the questions. If that is true, this is probably a great accomplishment for him to tackle the complexity of the readings. It may very well be that he understood the readings but could not answer the questions because they contained vocabulary that he had not yet mastered.

The way memory works in the situation follows:

1. The student reads the selections. While reading, his working memory, the space in his brain behind his forehead, holds on to the new information, while drawing on long-term memories previously stored to help him comprehend what he reads.

2. When he reads the questions that relate to the selections he has just read, he must be able to understand the vocabulary of the question so well that he doesn't utilize any of the working memory space that is now designated as a holding port for the comprehension of the reading selections.

3. The student should automatically know and comprehend what the question is asking without skipping a beat. If the question is not understood, a few different situations can follow. First, he might

ponder the wording of the question. In the scenario, the word was *analyze*. He could sit there and say to himself, *"Analyze. What is that? I know I have heard it before. But how do I analyze something?"* Now, he either figures out what it means and returns to the test, or he does not and the answer is blank. If the former occurs—that is, how to analyze suddenly comes to mind—he now must go back and figure out again what he is analyzing. You see, he pushed some of that information out of his working memory as he tried to figure out the definition of the word. And time keeps on ticking. . . .

The second observation of the scenario with Michael is the fact that he is looking down. If you are familiar with eye-accessing cues as described by Ruby Payne (2009), you know that when we look down we are accessing our feelings rather than our memories. As long as Michael is looking down, feeling badly that he doesn't understand what he is to do, and perhaps feeling like he is "dumb," he cannot access the definition of the word *analyze*. He must look up to get the visualizations he may have stored from learning the word, so the first thing to do with a Michael situation in your classroom is to walk over to him and ask him a question that forces him to look up at you. That could trigger a memory.

If They Process It, It Will Be Stored

Memory is processed in a way that on paper looks very linear. The brain is, however, a parallel processor, and the brain can store information in different systems and structures simultaneously.

Typically, a long-term memory is formed by information passing through several systems. First, information enters the brain through the senses (visual, auditory, kinesthetic, olfactory, or gustatory). This information first must be noticed by the sensory memory system. If that occurs, the information is now in immediate or conscious memory, where it will last up to 30 seconds. If the information is acted upon in any way, it will be placed in working memory. From working memory, which can last for hours, with enough engagements, the material may become long-term memories. It is in those working memory actions that networks in the brain are created and reinforced.

For students like Michael, extra processing of academic vocabulary words is necessary. The fact may be that many of our students have heard these important terms and have done assignments using these important terms, but for one reason or another, there wasn't enough processing time for their particular memory systems to store the words in long-term nonmotor procedural memory.

Here is the plan: process the critical words in enough different ways to get them stored in the brain in multiple places. The result of this is easier access to the definition. Continue to rehearse the processing in enough formats over time, and the words become as automatic as who, what, why, how, and where!

As Eric Jensen says (in a 2012 webinar from Scientific Learning, "Teaching with the Brain in Mind"), "Don't teach it 'til they get it right—teach it until they can't get it wrong!"

CHAPTER 3

The Critical Words: The Verbs

These words constitute the vocabulary of the CCSS. They are the words that are contained within the anchor standards and grade-level standards, and they are the words that are used in the exemplars provided by the Common Core authors. PARCC, the Partnership for Assessment for Readiness of College and Careers, is a consortium of 23 states plus the U.S. Virgin Islands working together to develop a common set of K–12 assessments in English and math anchored in what it takes to be ready for college and careers. A 7th grade sample has recently been placed on their website:

Grade 7 Prose Constructed Response from Research Simulation Task (Summary)

Student Directions

Based on the information in the text "Biography of Amelia Earhart," write an essay that summarizes and explains the challenges Earhart faced throughout her life.

Remember to use textual evidence to support your ideas.

(Available at: http://www.parcconline.org/samples/english-language-artsliteracy/grade-7-prose-constructed-response-research-simulation-task)

As you can see, three of the critical words are present in these directions: *summarize, explain,* and *support.*

In an explanation of the end-of-year assessment, they state, "On the end-of-year assessment, students have the opportunity to demonstrate their ability to read and comprehend complex informational and literary texts." Two more critical words: *demonstrate* and *comprehend.*

More Than Just "Standard" Vocabulary

The first consideration for choosing these words was the Common Core State Standards. It makes perfect sense to teach students what they are expected to know and be able to do. I also looked at the cognitive domain of Bloom's taxonomy, both original (Bloom, 1956) and revised (Anderson & Krathwohl, 2001). Bloom's is a taxonomy of thinking skills. In addition, I selected Norman Webb's Depth of Knowledge levels as a measurement for many of the words. Webb's DOK, as it is often called, looks at the cognitive demand or expectation of a task.

Bloom's Revised Taxonomy

Level of Thinking: Remember
Recognize information stored in memory; recall information stored in memory

Level of Thinking: Understand
Interpret; summarize; show examples; classify; infer; compare; explain

Level of Thinking: Apply
Execute knowledge

Level of Thinking: Analyze
Differentiate; organize; attribute

Level of Thinking: Evaluate
Check; critique

Level of Thinking: Create
Generate; plan; produce

Webb's DOK

Level 1: Recall
Recall of a fact, information, or procedure; rote response; follow a set procedure; typically involves one step

Level 2: Basic Reasoning
Use information or conceptual knowledge; make decisions about how to approach the question or problem; use two or more steps that go beyond recall or simple procedure

Level 3: Strategic Thinking
Requires reasoning, developing a plan or sequence of steps; has some complexity; more than one possible answer based on more demanding reasoning

Level 4: Extended Thinking
Requires an investigation, time to think and process multiple conditions of the problem or task; relate ideas within and among content

Some of the critical words are important in all three categories: standards, Bloom, and Webb's DOK. Some words may be low on Bloom but require more cognitive demand on a certain level of Webb's. This is all information to help you decide how important the word is to you at your grade level. I believe that all children must know the critical verbs as these will appear throughout school and life. Many of the critical nouns fall into that same category, but there are a few that you may want to wait to teach at a higher grade level.

Pre-assess

You may want to begin with a pre-assessment in order to determine whether you need to cover all of the verbs. Figure 3.1 is a possible pre-assessment. Students can simply place a check mark in the appropriate column, or you may want them to write a definition in the "I might Know It" and "I Know It!" columns.

FIGURE 3.1
A Pre-Assessment for the Critical Verbs

Word	I don't know it	I might know it	I know it!
Analyze			
Articulate			
Cite			
Compare			
Comprehend			
Contrast			
Delineate			
Demonstrate			
Describe			
Determine			
Develop			
Distinguish			
Draw			
Evaluate			
Explain			
Identify			
Infer			
Integrate			
Interpret			
Locate			
Organize			
Paraphrase			
Refer			
Retell			
Suggest			
Summarize			
Support			
Synthesize			
Trace			

How Important Are These Words?

Take a look at the first word, *analyze*. If you read the Anchor Standards, you will see that the verb *analyze* is used in the College and Career Readiness Anchor Standards for Reading in Standards 2, 3, 4, 5, and 9. In Anchor Standard 2, the student must "analyze the development of that central idea or theme." *Analyze* also appears in Anchor Standard 3: "Analyze how and why individuals, events, and ideas develop and interact over the course of a text." In Anchor Standard 4, the student must "analyze how specific word choices shape meaning or tone." And in Anchor Standard 5, the student must "analyze the structure of text." Finally, anchor Standard 9 begins with "Analyze how two or more texts address similar themes or topics."

Many of the words are interconnected—you need one critical word to define another critical word. As you'll see later in this chapter, in the definitions of the words, any words marked with an * are on the critical word list.

The Verbs

I have divided the critical words into a list of nouns and verbs. Because the verbs contain the action of the standards and the nouns are often the receivers of the action, it makes sense to begin with the verbs. If one considers the concept-based learning suggested for differentiated instruction, the verbs are the "Do's" (what students are expected to be able to do). Once the students master the verbs and have them stored permanently in long-term memory, those actions can be used in various situations for practice. For instance, it would behoove you to begin using those verbs in your questioning, on quizzes, and on other classroom assessments.

According to Willis (2006), p. 29:

> When the brain perceives information repeated in multiple ways, there is a *priming* process that makes encoding of that information more efficient. That is why writing a vocabulary word in a sentence, hearing classmates read their sentences, and then following the direction to use the word in conversation during that day will result

in more successful long-term memory storage and retrieval than just memorizing the definition (Koutstaal et al., 1997).

We have to make these words brain-compatible in order to make the brain core-compatible. This will include using many, if not all, of the following techniques:

1. Vocabulary word maps: these are essential to students understanding variations of the words, synonyms, antonyms, examples, non-examples, how to use them in sentences, and how to picture them in their minds. The Frayer model can be used as its own vocabulary word map or in addition to another map (Frayer, Frederick, & Klausmeier, 1969).

2. Mind mapping is a procedure that appeals to many students. Since we have 55 words to teach the students, variety is necessary. Mind mapping will be explained in a later chapter (D'Antoni, Zipp, & Olson, 2009).

3. Paper foldables are excellent sources for students to create a vocabulary word booklet (Dye, 2000).

4. Vocabulary word gloves provides students with a way to use movement to study the words alone or in groups.

5. Check My Vocabulary cards will be a way to get the entire faculty and staff on board with this project of making learning these critical words an event.

6. Jingles! Many students require rhythm and rhyme to assist with their memories. I provide a jingle for each word, but your students may want to make up their own.

7. Vocabulary cartoons may help students remember words.

8. Movement activities such as Freeze Frame, skits, and puppet shows make learning fun.

9. Analogies can be used to reinforce meaning and to assist students in making meaning of their own (Marzano, Pickering, & Pollack, 2001).

10. Internet sites will be helpful in making personal definitions, finding pictures to represent words, and locating antonyms and synonyms.

These are just 10 of the strategies that will be explained and modeled in this book.

Our goals must be clear:

1. To teach the critical words in ways that help each student store them in long-term memory
2. To make the words instantly recognizable
3. To make the meanings of the words accessible automatically
4. To keep working memory space available for acting on the word by combining prior knowledge and new information from the text, selection, or assessment

The Critical Verbs

The following section contains the verbs and suggestions for teaching each one (see Figure 3.2 for a list of the verbs and their definitions). There is no magic to each strategy. The magic is getting these into memory. Teach these words in ways that are comfortable for you. You will find an appendix in the back of this book with reproducibles; however, keep in mind that if your students create their own vocabulary word maps or Venn diagrams, they will remember the content on them better.

- Use one of your learning centers as a vocabulary center for the critical words.
- Use the beginning of the day or of class to spend a few minutes on a word.
- Have a word wall with the critical words.
- Use the gradual release of responsibility model as you teach the words.

Order of the Introduction of the Critical Verbs

You may be asking, "With which verb do I begin?" Although the words are in alphabetical order in this book to make them easier to find, the following list shows the verbs according to the grade level in which they are introduced in the Common Core State Standards for English Language Arts/Literacy

FIGURE 3.2
The Critical Verbs and Their Definitions

Verb	Definition
Analyze	Break something down into its parts
Articulate	Express clearly
Cite	Quote
Compare	Find likenesses
Comprehend	Understand; find meaning
Contrast	Find differences
Delineate	Describe in detail
Demonstrate	Show clearly
Describe	Tell the facts, details
Determine	Decide
Develop	Elaborate or expand
Distinguish	Set apart
Draw	Take or pull out
Evaluate	Find value; judge
Explain	Make plain or define
Identify	Find; point out
Infer	Deduce; conclude
Integrate	Put together
Interpret	Explain the meaning of
Locate	Find
Organize	Arrange; classify
Paraphrase	Put in different words
Refer	Mention
Retell	Tell in your own words
Suggest	Put forth; to say
Summarize	Sum up
Support	Hold up
Synthesize	Combine to form a more complex product
Trace	Outline; follow the course of

or in the standards' Appendix B: Text Exemplars and Sample Performance Tasks. Remember that your students must eventually store all of these words in memory. If you are a 3rd grade teacher, be sure that your students have mastered the kindergarten, 1st, and 2nd grade words as well.

- Kindergarten: *compare, contrast, describe, distinguish, identify, retell*
- 1st: *demonstrate, determine, draw, explain, locate, suggest, support*
- 2nd: *comprehend, develop*
- 3rd: *organize, refer*
- 4th: *infer, integrate, interpret, paraphrase, summarize*
- 5th: *analyze*
- 6th: *articulate, cite, delineate, evaluate, trace*
- 11th: *synthesize*

So, 28 of the 29 verbs in this chapter must be mastered by 6th grade.

What Do They Know: Differentiation

You will want to differentiate your instruction as your classroom may be quite diverse. At some point you want your students to be able to fill in the following chart or one similar to it. Figure 3.3 is a formative assessment to use to differentiate the critical verbs.

Although the table includes all of the verbs, you will probably want to use this type of assessment with smaller groups of words as you teach them. I have tried to fill this book with strategies that you can use to teach these critical words and all vocabulary. You are the expert in your classroom and have many tried and true strategies that you use regularly. Adding new strategies is what we do as we try to keep our teacher toolboxes filled to the brim and keep our teaching fresh and interesting. I hope you find some of these strategies helpful.

I have grouped some of the verbs. This does not mean that they must be taught together; rather, they are linked together as skills, and they are often compared. Examples of these groups include *compare* and *contrast*, and *paraphrase* and *summarize*.

FIGURE 3.3
Formative Assessment to Differentiate Teaching of the Critical Verbs

Word	My definition	My sentence using this word
Analyze		
Articulate		
Cite		
Compare		
Comprehend		
Contrast		
Delineate		
Demonstrate		
Describe		
Determine		
Develop		
Distinguish		
Draw		
Evaluate		
Explain		
Identify		
Infer		
Integrate		
Interpret		
Locate		
Organize		
Paraphrase		
Refer		
Retell		
Suggest		
Summarize		
Support		
Synthesize		
Trace		

The activities in this book are about student engagement. Your students do not need worksheets handed to them. Have students work together to create or fill out graphic organizers. Graphic organizers are a step between what the teacher or the text says and what will become long-term memory for the student.

The Critical Verb Song

The following song is sung or chanted to the tune of the "Military Count-Off Song," which begins with

I don't know, but I've been told
Air force wings are made of gold!

The purpose of the song is to give students familiarity with the verbs themselves. It may be useful to have students sing it as they transition from one subject to another.

Analyze, articulate, don't you think this song is great?
Cite, compare, and comprehend, will it never, ever end?
Contrast and delineate, I'll go on to demonstrate.
Describe, determine, and develop, do you want to give it up?
Distinguish, draw, evaluate, verbs to love and never hate.
Explain, identify, infer, important words you must concur!
Integrate, interpret, locate. Learn them before it is too late.
Organize and paraphrase, use them right and receive praise.
Refer, retell, and suggest are words that will be on the test.
Support, summarize, synthesize, and trace. Learn these verbs and tests you'll ace.

How to Read and Understand the Standards and Exemplars

In most instances in this book, I have written out the standards that I am referring to. For instance, I may say, "Anchor Standard 9 in the College and Career Readiness Anchors for Reading states. . . ." For the grade-level standards, I may write, "Under Reading Standards for Literature K–5, the first grade-level standards for grades 3 and 4 students begin with

1. Ask and answer questions to demonstrate understanding of a text, referring explicitly to the text as the basis for the answers.
2. Refer to details and examples in a text when explaining what the text says explicitly and when drawing inferences from the text.

In some cases, you will see initials and letters after a standard as in [RL.K.7] This stands for Reading Literature for Kindergarten, grade-level standard 7. After examples from Appendix B, you will always see a bracketed standard and grade-level abbreviation. This is to indicate to you the grade level and type of standard. Examples might be [RI.2.1] meaning Reading Informational Text, Grade 2, Grade level standard 1, or you may see [RH.6–8.1] referring to Reading Standards for Literacy in History and Social Studies, Grade levels 6–8, Grade level standard 1. The abbreviation RST stands for Reading in Science and Technical Subjects, SL is for Speaking and Listening, and W is for Writing.

Also, please note that the emphases in the Appendix B exemplars are mine. I simply italicized only the critical word for a clearer understanding.

Analyze

Definition: break something down into its parts

Synonyms: examine, study, scrutinize, explore

🎵 **Jingle:**   An-a-lyze, break it down, down, down,
          Then explain what you found, found, found.

Analyze in the Common Core

The first word alphabetically also happens to be one of the most common words in the standards. You will find it no less than 70 times! *Analyze* is a vocabulary word that appears initially in the 5th grade standards and is then used throughout the rest of the grade levels.

Play on Words

Analyze means to examine critically, so as to bring out the essential elements or give the essence of: to analyze a poem. (http://dictionary.reference.com/browse/analyze?s=t)

Not all of the critical words will easily become a play on words, but *analyze* does: Anna lies.

> *Because Anna lies, we have to analyze what she says to find out what is true.*
>
> *What happens to Pinocchio when he lies?*

Vocabulary Word Map

The research suggests that many students gain insight from using graphic organizers. An organizer is not a worksheet—it is a way to put semantic information into a picture that is easy to remember. Figure 3.4 shows one type of vocabulary word map using the word *analyze.*

FIGURE 3.4
Vocabulary Word Map for Using *Analyze*

Write the word.	analyze
Write a definition of the word.	break down
Write a synonym.	examine
Write an antonym.	
Write the word here, in color.	
Use the word in a sentence that shows its meaning.	
Draw a picture showing the meaning of the word.	

Vocabulary Word Gloves

The Vocabulary Gloves can be set up in various ways. I buy inexpensive work gloves and thin permanent markers. Each pair of gloves is good for two vocabulary words. The word goes on the outside of the glove, and I hang the gloves with a hook on a clothesline. During vocabulary time, students can grab a glove and work on a particular word. I have this pair set up with the definition on the thumb, several synonyms on the first three fingers, and an antonym on the pinky. In the middle I have the word used in a sentence. Students can quiz each other on the words using the gloves, or they can quiz themselves. See the Vocabulary Word Gloves in Figure 3.5.

FIGURE 3.5
Vocabulary Word Gloves Using *Analyze*

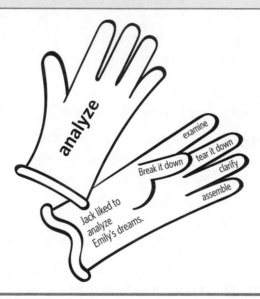

Check My Vocabulary!

This activity involves staff and faculty outside the classroom. When a student seems to have mastered the critical word, he or she is offered the opportunity to take the card and visit someone like the principal, custodian, media specialist, or anyone else who has agreed to participate. The student finds the participant and asks, "May I show you how well I know the word *analyze*?" If it is an opportune time, he or she hands the card over and waits to be quizzed. See Figure 3.6 for a sample card.

FIGURE 3.6
Sample Check My Vocabulary Card for *Analyze*

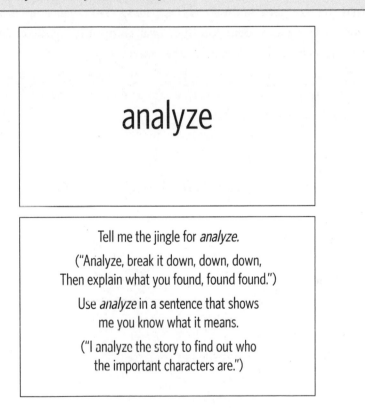

This figure is just an example of what can go on the cards. One of the important components of this activity is that it gives the student the opportunity to show off to someone, gives him or her confidence, and allows him or her to use the information outside the classroom.

3-D Graphic Organizer

Many different types of graphic organizers are available on the Internet and in the books of Dinah Zike (1992). Students enjoy making these organizers and may want to choose a different one than the one that I am going to share.

Tri-fold Booklet: This organizer is simple to make by taking a sheet of paper (I like to use colored construction paper and let the kids pick the color they like) and folding it in thirds.

Fold the right side in first and then the left side over it, so it opens like a brochure. I have the students put the vocabulary word on the cover and draw a picture to help them understand the word.

When the student opens the brochure, the back of the third section is showing. Here, I have students write a sentence using the word. There are three spaces on the inside of the brochure. They may be used for a defintion, synonyms, or another picture or icon using the word. On the back of the brochure, students can write a question using the word with multiple possible answers.

Sentence: The scientists analyze the formula and discover the ingredients are ethyl alcohol, water, and sodium.

Defintion: [This would be the student definition, *not* a dictionary definition.]

Synonyms: examine

Back: If you analyze a story, you could find the following:
   a. The setting, characters, and theme
   b. How you feel about the author
   c. The summary

As you move on to the other critical words, you will find some similar strategies, as well as some that are a bit different. Not all students will need to use every strategy; however, some of your learners will need to learn in mutliple ways to get this information into long-term, automatic memory.

Technology: visit www.dictionary.com for defintions, synonyms, and antonyms.

Articulate

Definition: Express clearly

Example: Joey writes and speaks eloquently. He articulates well.

🎵 **Jingle**:   Articulate and say it well,
Be as clear as a bell.

Articulate in the Common Core

In their portrait of what students who meet the standards can do, the CCSS state that students should be able to "build on others' ideas, *articulate* their own idea" (Introduction, p. 7, http://www.corestandards.org/assets/CCSSI_ELA%20Standards.pdf).

In the exemplars found in Appendix B of the CCSS, the use of *articulate* begins in grade 6 and is used through grade 12.

Keyword Mnemonic

This method helps students create a visual image to help them remember the word. *Anticipate* sounds similar to *articulate*.

Jimmy anticipates that he will need to articulate when selling papers.
Anticipate that you'll articulate.
Trayvon articulated his understanding of the story.

Freeze Frame

Students are put in pairs and are given a few minutes to come up with a scene that explains the meaning of *articulate*. In this activity they must stand like statues.

Mind Map

1. In the middle of a sheet of paper, have students PRINT their vocabulary word—in this case, *articulate*. Then have them draw a circle around the word with markers or colored pens.
2. Students draw lines coming out of the circle like spokes on a wheel.
3. On the lines, students write synonyms for the word.
4. They may also make a picture or icon to go with each word. See Figure 3.7.

FIGURE 3.7
A Mind Map for the Word *Articulate*

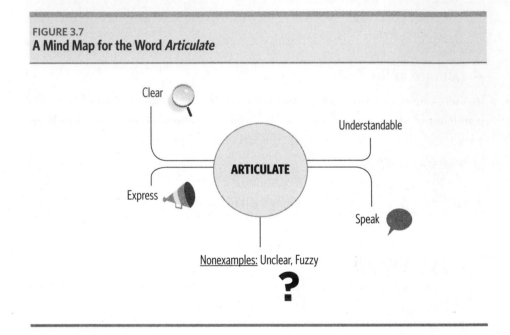

Frayer Model

The Frayer model (Frayer, Frederick, & Klausmeier, 1969) is a graphic organizer that works well with vocabulary words. It is much like the vocabulary word map used for *articulate*. I like the Frayer model with the example and nonexample sections (see Figure 3.8). I would also ask students to draw a picture of the word at some point.

FIGURE 3.8
Frayer Model for the Word *Articulate*

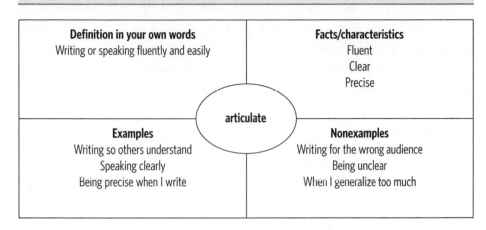

Definition in your own words	Facts/characteristics
Writing or speaking fluently and easily	Fluent Clear Precise

articulate

Examples	Nonexamples
Writing so others understand Speaking clearly Being precise when I write	Writing for the wrong audience Being unclear When I generalize too much

Cite

Definition: note, quote, refer to, point out

Synonyms: quote, name, mention

🎵 **Jingle:**   Cite is about
Pointing things out!

Movement: A simple movement or kinesthetic activity to go along with this word is placing your hands as though they are binoculars and putting them up to your eyes.

Keyword Mnemonic: This strategy is similar to a play on words. Use a word that is similar to the critical word to help students relate to the word and remember it.

Keyword: sight

- Set your sight on cite.
- Can you cite reasons to see the sights?

Concept Map

Concept maps are used to show students how concepts relate to one another. Have students create a concept map using the word *cite* (see the example in Figure 3.9). Begin with *cite* at the top of the paper. Keep in mind that this can be done using computers or tablets and programs such as Kidspiration.

As students discuss and brainstorm the word, they can write key words below *cite* and draw arrows to make connections among the ideas.

FIGURE 3.9
A Concept Map Using the Critical Verb *Cite*

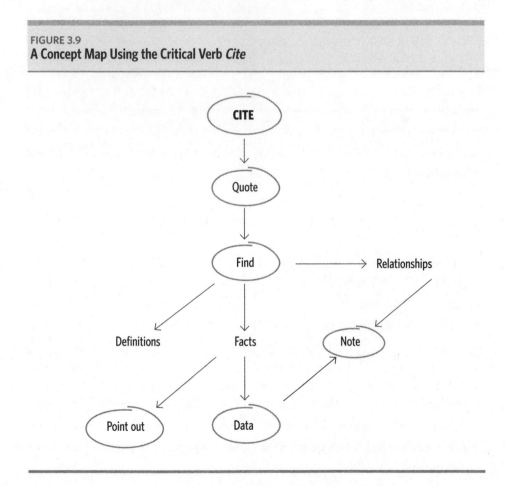

I Draw! You Draw!

In this activity, the teacher draws a picture or icon representing *cite*. For instance, I might simply put up large quotation marks, "_____," as my symbol for the word to remind myself that *cite* can mean *quote*.

The students then draw their own icon or picture of the word without anyone ever saying that the word we are drawing is *cite*. Students can then share pictures and exchange ideas about how the picture helps them remember the word.

Table for Two

In this activity, students create a simple two-column table. The heading for the first column is "Word," while the second is "Drawing." Students write the critical verb in the first column and a picture depicting that word in the second column. This is a short review activity using a number of the critical words already used.

Picture Wall

If you already have a word wall with the critical words you have studied thus far, take down the words and replace them with pictures the students have drawn or found that represent the words. You can do this activity in teams or individually. The teacher gently throws a bean bag toward a picture, and the student or team must come up with the word that picture represents. If it is easy to take down the picture, the team or student can have the picture until the end of the game. The team or student who guesses the word correctly gets to throw the bean bag next. This activity can be done with several pictures representing the same word, so you don't have to have studied many words to make this a fun game. Remember, repetition is good for the brain and memory!

Compare/Contrast

Compare

Definition: find likenesses between two or more things

🎵 **Jingle:**   Compare to find things the same,
See how many you can name!

Movement: Put hands together with fingers spread, indicating the sameness of the fingers on each hand.

Contrast

Definition: find differences between two or more things

🎵 **Jingle:**   Contrast to find different things
See how many you can bring!

Compare and *Contrast* in the Common Core

These critical words are used in the kindergarten standards and throughout the grade-level standards of the CCSS. You will find the need for comparative thinking in the CCSS such as RL.K.9 (Reading Literature, Kindergarten) and 2.NBT.4 (Mathematics, Grade 2, Numbers and Operations in Base 10) If our kindergarteners get critical words like these into nonmotor procedural long-term memory, it will improve their test scores as well as improve their ability to understand and do classwork. The icing on the cake, so to speak, is that these are life skill words that they will use forever!

Compare and *contrast* is a strategy by which students can read multiple texts and analyze them.

Anchor Standard 9 in the College and Career Readiness Anchors for Reading states:

9. Analyze how two or more texts address similar themes or topics in order to build knowledge or to *compare* the approaches the authors take.

Teaching *Compare* and *Contrast*

I am not suggesting that you teach these important verbs at the same time. I am presenting them this way because *contrast* usually follows *compare* in most curriculums. It helps some students to remember these words better when they are compared and contrasted using graphic organizers like Venn diagrams.

I walk in the 8th grade classroom wearing my Mickey Mouse costume. I certainly have the students' attention. The theme to *The Mickey Mouse Club* television show is playing in the background. I introduce myself as Mickey and ask the students what they know about me. Some of the students have been to Disneyland and share their experiences. As some of them refer to other Disney characters, I reach into my closet and bring out a large Donald Duck stuffed toy. Soon the students are talking about Donald, although it is clear that many know little about him.

I have the students do a think-pair-share about the characters. This gives the students a break from listening to me and allows them to move around and gather information from their classmates. (See, I am doing all the right things and I am quite pleased with the way things are going.)

I explain to the students when they return to their seats that we are going to learn how to "compare and contrast" the Disney characters. I ask for definitions of the words. Some students look them up in their dictionaries, while others use a search engine on the computers in the classroom. We discuss the definitions for a few minutes.

Together, the students and I begin to write a paragraph comparing Mickey and Donald. When we complete the paragraph and the students have copied it into their notebooks, we begin to discuss the story we are reading. The two main characters are brothers, and they are perfect for the class to write about in a compare/contrast paragraph. As I walk around the room to check on substance and form, some of my students are staring at blank pages. I advise them to look at the paragraph we have written about Mickey and Donald and model their paragraphs after it. I remind them that they are looking for things that are alike between the brothers and things that are different. Most students get busy after my explanation.

As we continued to work on this kind of writing and thinking, the students used Venn diagrams and T-charts to help them understand. Still, many of them did not internalize the skill and associate it with the correct vocabulary. When the state test was given and my students were asked to compare or contrast, some of them did not answer correctly or at all because they did not know what the questions were asking of them.

The ability to do comparative thinking or comparative analysis has been shown by researchers (Marzano et al., 2001) to raise student achievement up to 45 percentile points. This is amazing and makes sense when you consider the way the brain functions. Comparing and contrasting is the process used by the brain to clarify our world. It is the lens through which our students learn. The brain takes in information and asks, "What is this like? Is this like something else I have encountered? How is this different than that? What do I need to know to understand this?"

Sesame Street knows the importance of children being able to compare items. In their "Which of these things is not like the other?" segment, they are asking young brains to find likenesses and differences. Although this sounds like a simple task, it is the beginning of asking higher-level questions like "What should I compare? What characteristics are important? What things are the same or different? To what level do I take this comparison?"

When I teach this concept to teachers, so they can adapt it to the grade level they teach, I always begin with a list of words for them to categorize or classify. These processes promote the skill of comparison. What is fun about this is that I can choose just about any words, and the teachers discover what types of characteristics are important to them.

For instance, my list may contain *trees, billboards, war, politics, insurance, automobiles, grain elevators, global positioning systems (GPS), anger, Japan, toys,* and *dogs.* How would you classify these words? What headings would you use? I had one group of teachers who used the following categories: Government and Trips. Did you come up with more? Read the explanation these teachers gave:

- When you take a trip, you might drive an automobile and along the way see trees and billboards. If you see trees and billboards when you are expecting to see malls and casinos, you better get out your GPS and find out where you are! If you have kids, you better bring plenty of toys for them to play with as they get bored easily. Many of their toys may be made in Japan. You have to decide if you want to take the dog with you. If you do, those trees may come in handy!

- It makes us angry when we think about the politics involved in our government. War seems to be such a waste of resources. You better take out an insurance policy on any of your loved ones who are going off to war.

The similarities we find are based on our own personal experiences in the real world and from prior knowledge we have gained through academics. Of course, some students have more background experience than others.

Signal Words

Sometimes *compare* means *compare* and sometimes *compare* means *compare and contrast*. Teach students the signal words for each skill. Share essays with them in which they can underline the signal words. Also, have the students write their own papers comparing two texts or two essays, and ask them to underline the signal words they use.

Signal words for compare: *similarly, and, likewise, just as . . . so, both, comparatively, each, can be compared, alike, same, also*

Signal words for contrast: *however, still, but, yet, nevertheless, instead, even though, on the contrary, although, though, on the other hand, despite, conversely, different from, each, whereas, neither . . . nor, while, either . . . or, more, less than, then . . . now, one . . . the other*

Many teachers introduce these two vocabulary words together, so many of the graphic organizers are set up for both similarities and differences. I like to give students options. Some want to fill in a premade graphic organizer, but others remember much more if they create a mind map or concept map.

Venn Diagram

This graphic organizer is often used to teach *compare* and *contrast*. Drawn easily by students, it is an effective way for students to see how two people, items, or ideas are similar and different (see Figure 3.10). The outer parts of the circles contain characteristics that are different, while the overlap of the circles in the center contains the similarities.

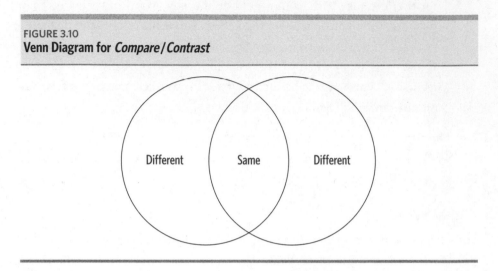

FIGURE 3.10
Venn Diagram for *Compare / Contrast*

T-Chart

Students simply draw a large T on paper. One side is for similarities and the other for differences (see Figure 3.11).

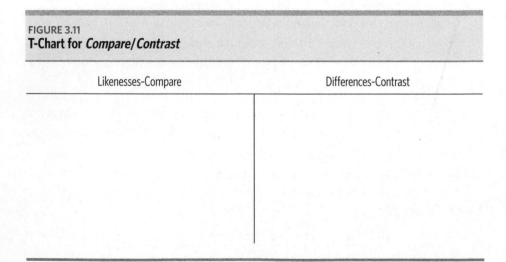

FIGURE 3.11
T-Chart for *Compare/Contrast*

Likenesses-Compare	Differences-Contrast

Vocabulary Word Map

These maps can be done in many ways. Figure 3.12 shows a different version of a vocabulary word map for the word *compare* that varies from one used on page 35.

FIGURE 3.12
Vocabulary Word Map for *Compare*

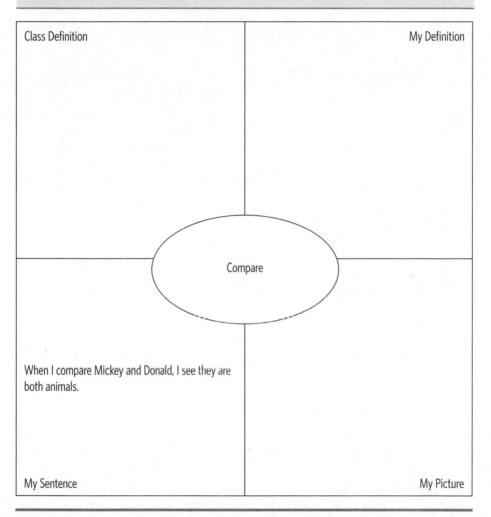

Compare/Contrast Organizer

Venn diagrams do not always provide enough space for differences so you may want to use another graphic organizer. Figure 3.13 is an organizer that works well with *compare/contrast*.

FIGURE 3.13
Compare/Contrast **Graphic Organizer**

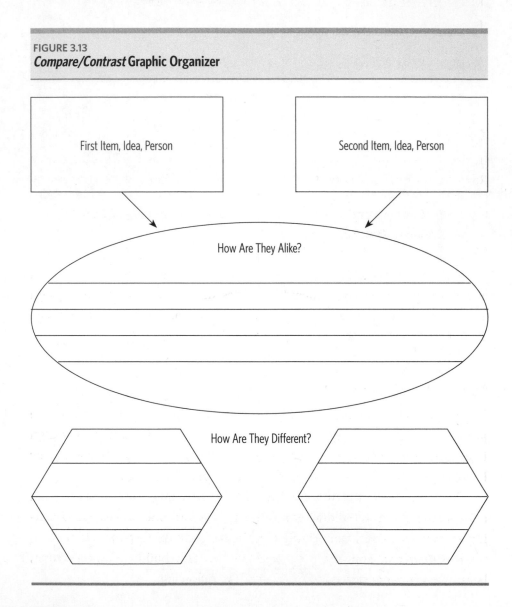

Comprehend

Definition: get the picture, understand, dig it, grasp, catch on, find meaning

🎵 **Jingle:**   Comprehend, can you dig it?

Movement: Act like you have a shovel and dig.

Comprehend in the Common Core

In the College and Career Readiness Anchor Standards for Reading under Range of Reading and Level of Text Complexity, Anchor Standard 10 reads:

10. Read and *comprehend* complex literary and informational texts independently and proficiently.

It is expected that by the end of 2nd grade, students will be able to read and comprehend literature, including stories, dramas, and poetry, at the high end of the grades 2–3 text complexity band independently and proficiently. This expectation is extended at each grade level.

Teaching *Comprehend*

The RAND Reading Study Group (2002) stated that *comprehension* is "the process of simultaneously extracting and constructing meaning through interaction and involvement with written language" (p. 11). Through prior knowledge and experience, readers construct knowledge from text.

Teachers help students comprehend by teaching various skills such as decoding, fluency, building and activating background knowledge, teaching vocabulary words, and helping them make personal responses to text.

Knowing and applying every verb in this text builds comprehension, because comprehension consists of all of the following:

- Articulating what you understand
- Analyzing text
- Citing important information
- Supporting conclusions
- Understanding comparisons
- Drawing information from what you have read
- Evaluating text and your own conclusions
- Identifying important information like main ideas and evidence
- Making inferences
- Interpreting text
- Organizing your own thoughts and understanding the organization of a text
- Synthesizing information
- Summarizing or paraphrasing what an author has said
- Locating valuable information
- Developing your own ideas and capturing what an author has developed

In short, comprehension is what you teach when you teach the critical verbs and nouns. Therefore, every strategy that you use in this book, from graphic organizers to jingles to movement, helps to build your students' comprehension. The trick is to use the word *comprehend* and its derivatives (transformations).

Ask students questions using the word *comprehend:*

"Do you comprehend what the author is saying?"

In *The Giver,* does Jonah comprehend the enormity of his responsibility?"

Mind Map

Mind-mapping *comprehend* may help students understand it a bit better. It will put some pictures in their minds (see Figure 3.14).

Can you dig it?

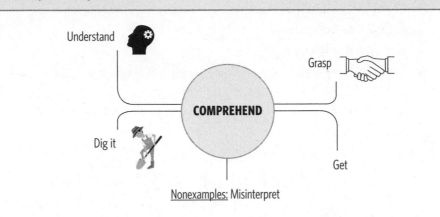

FIGURE 3.14
Mind Map for *Comprehend*

Delineate

Definition: describe in detail; outline

Synonyms: outline, describe*, define

Several of the critical words are synonyms (see asterisks above). However, each word must get into long-term nonmotor procedural memory, so we must teach each word separately. Many of your students will begin to make the connections and wonder why they need to know all of those words that mean the same thing or are similar. Explain to them that all of these words are in the standards, and that no one knows which word will appear in a text, on an assessment, or in conversation. From retelling a story as a kindergartner to being interviewed for a job, these will come up often for your students.

♫ **Jingle:**   Delineate uses words to show
                1, 2, 3, what you know.

Movement: Outline one hand with the index finger of the other hand.

Examples:
- On maps, different colors are used to delineate the territories of countries and states.
- Some children are not able to delineate between good and bad behavior.

Play on Words:
- Delineate "Dee Lynn he ate!"
- The gorilla was able to delineate the outline of her body and then Dee Lynn he ate!

Teaching *Delineate*

If you have not begun a word wall with the critical words, this may be a good time to do so. Some of the critical words are almost synonymous, and it is important to help students discover which words can be interchanged. It is still very important to teach the students each word, its jingle, and definition, because telling them that *delineate* could be used instead of *describe* often confuses the issue. Students must be able to recognize each word when they encounter it on an assessment, but it will reinforce the learning if the students understand that some of the words have similar meanings. A website like dictionary.com, which has both a dictionary and a thesaurus, might be a great way for your students to discover synonyms.

A keyword mnemonic is helpful with this critical word. I found using the word *determinate,* which is not used often and rhymes with *delineate,* helps students create a visual image for memory storage. Visual image processing is helpful for most students, and the brain has a natural tendency to store pictures (Medina, 2008). As students relate to the sentence below, they will form a picture, perhaps of themselves receiving allowance for work done.

Dad will delineate Jack's chores in order to determinate his allowance.

Students can draw a picture of father and son talking, and then make a list of chores such as:

1. Make bed
2. Take out garbage
3. Rake leaves

Vocabulary Gloves

I like using the glove for words that are new for many students. It will provide them practice independently or at learning centers. Here are examples of what could be on the gloves:

Palm: Sentence
In my report I will delineate the steps taken in the robbery.

Thumb: Definition
outline

Index finger: synonym
describe

Middle finger: synonym
define

Ring finger: synonym
describe

Pinky: antonym
misrepresent; twist

Have the students outline their hands on plain paper and discuss how they can trace or delineate solid objects. Then continue the discussion with ways that we delineate what we have read.

Colorful Delineation

Have students read a short selection that is part of the regular curriculum that you are studying. As they make an outline of the selection, ask them to delineate the various ideas or themes by using different-colored markers or pencils. This will help them get a visual picture of what the word means in direct relation to their deeper reading of the text.

3-D Graphic Organizer

Paper folding is fun for students, and using a graphic organizer that has three dimensions can be a nice change for your students. Use construction or colored paper, and allow your students to choose their color. Ask them to fold their paper hamburger-style. That is, fold the top of the paper down to the bottom and crease it in the center. The purpose of this organizer is to have the students write about the word *delineate* in outline form. Tell them they will be delineating *delineate*. That should be fun to say. Be sure to have them repeat the jingle when they hear the word *delineate* to reinforce the word and definition.

As they look at their folded paper, the crease should be at the top. Ask them to write the word *delineate* on the cover in whatever color they choose. If you have the time, they could print out the word in a colorful or fancy font. Then have students lift the cover. They are now going to write an outline for *delineate.* They may put the information for Roman numeral I in the upper half of the inside of the organizer, and Roman numeral II and its information on the bottom.

I. To describe in detail
    A. Outline
    B. Details
II. Order
    A. First, next, finally
    B. Beginning, middle, end

They may draw a picture on the back of the organizer to help them remember. This outline may be a great way to delve into your content and explain how they would delineate it. For fiction, they would probably have a beginning, middle, and end; nonfiction might lend itself to steps that include first, next, and so forth. Refer to the section on text structure.

Demonstrate

Definition: describe or explain by examples

Synonyms: reveal, prove, explain, expound, display, operate, instruct, show, show off

♫ **Jingle:**   Demonstrate what you know,
Make it plain—Ready? Set. Go!

Movement: Students act as though they are showing someone how to build something. They mime taking a block and putting it in front of them. Then they add another and another during the "Ready? Set. Go!"

Examples:
- The flight attendant demonstrates how to buckle the seat belt.
- What have you seen others demonstrate?
- What can you demonstrate?
- Do you understand the story? What can you do to demonstrate what you know? (Retell the story, describe the action, tell about the story in order.)

Demonstrate According to Webb

When using Webb's (2005) Depth of Knowledge model to analyze the cognitive expectation demanded by standards, curricular activities, and assessment tasks, we find the word *demonstrate* in Level 1. Students will be asked to demonstrate their knowledge and understanding beginning in kindergarten.

Demonstrate in the Common Core

In the Common Core State Standards, students are expected to be able to do things like the following:

RL.1.2. Retell stories, including key details, and *demonstrate* understanding of their central message or lesson.

RL.2.1. Ask and answer such questions as who, what, where, when, why, and how to *demonstrate* understanding of key details in a text.

RI.3.1. Ask and answer questions to *demonstrate* understanding of a text, referring explicitly to the text as the basis for the answers.

PB & J

Many teachers begin teaching students the word *demonstrate* by doing a demonstration of something familiar like making a peanut butter and jelly sandwich. The lesson often continues by having students come up with something they can demonstrate in class the next day. Once the students understand *demonstrate* in this format, they move on to using *demonstrate* as a way of showing what they know or understand. They begin with oral demonstrations and then move to written ones.

Vocabulary Word Map

Use one of the sample maps in the appendix at the end of this book.

Be sure that students write the word in color. This will help students remember the word. Also in most maps, students will write the word at least three times:

1. In pen or pencil
2. In color
3. In the sentence

Vocabulary Gloves

Have vocabulary gloves available for the word *demonstrate*. You will need to differentiate instruction on many of the critical words. The gloves may be helpful for some of your flexible groups. Have them handy at a learning center.

Here are examples for your glove:

Palm: Sentence
I can demonstrate my understanding of the word by using it in a sentence.

Thumb: Definition
describe by examples

Index finger: synonym
describe

Middle finger: synonym
show

Ring finger: synonym
reveal

Pinky: antonym
hide

Describe

Definition: depict in words, tell in your own words

Synonyms: delineate*, portray, tell, explain*, report

♫ **Jingle:**   Describe and tell all about it.
                  Write it, share it, or even shout it!

Describe in Bloom and Webb

Although *describe* is considered a lower-level thinking skill according to the new Bloom's taxonomy, it can be found on all levels of Webb's Depth of Knowledge levels. The ability to describe ranges from describing simple features (Level 1) to describing themes found across texts (Level 4) (Webb, 2005).

     When you describe, you tell.

Lemon-aid

You may want to try this activity or something similar to introduce this important critical verb. To teach my students how to describe well, I used lemons. I would bring a bag or basket of lemons and either give each student a lemon or let them come up to my desk and pick one out. I gave them a few minutes to hold and look at the lemon before I asked them to bring the lemons back and place them back in the bag or basket.

After several minutes, I asked the students to come to the table one or two at a time and find their lemons. Almost none of the students knew which lemon they had been holding. I then gave each student a lemon again. This time I would tell them to name their lemon, spend some time looking at their lemon, and write a description of their lemon, but they were instructed to leave their names off their papers. When they completed these tasks, they returned their lemon to the table.

When all of the students completed the writing, I collected the descriptions and handed them out to random students. They read the descriptions and were asked to pick out the lemon that fit the description. This is an excellent way for them to see the importance of details. Although many of the students were able to find the correct lemon, some of the descriptions did not offer enough information.

Exit Cards

These cards are sometimes called "tickets to leave." These are index cards that the students fill out before they leave your class. The beauty of the critical words is that they are universal and will be used across content areas. All teachers can use the same or similar strategies.

The exit card generally has two or three questions or short activities for students to do about five minutes before dismissal. Then they turn the card in to you, and you receive a wealth of information about how well they are doing with getting these words and definitions into nonmotor procedural memory.

The steps to follow are something like this:

1. Pass out blank index cards.
2. Ask students to write down questions or activities such as these:
   Write the definition of the word *describe.*
   Write two synonyms for *describe.*
   Write an example of *describe* in a sentence.
3. Students take a few minutes to jot down answers.
4. You stand at the door and have them give you their ticket to leave as they are dismissed.

5. You go through the cards and see who knows the definition, or jingle, or synonyms, or whatever else you decide to ask.

This is an informal assessment and allows you to differentiate the study of the word according to how well the students know the information.

For the next class period, you may be able to group your students according to their memory of the word. Often you will have two or three groups. For the lowest group, you may use your learning centers. Have some students work with the vocabulary gloves, and have others work on the jingle. The middle group may just need to brush up on the way they use the word in a sentence. The group that really knows the word can review all of the words you have covered thus far, or they may create a vocabulary game with the words they know. ELL students and students who don't have the same background knowledge as the rest of the class may need more help. The jingles often benefit these students the most as the rhyming and rhythm may be the most powerful way to get the word and definition into memory. Drawing pictures or acting out the words is also helpful to these students.

Describe Anything!

Students who are having serious trouble with this word should be asked to describe things. Until they get the gist of the word, ask them to describe objects, clothing, and other tangible objects that they can see. Once they get that, move on to more abstract thinking such as describing the setting or characters in a story. Eventually move them to nonfiction text and ask them to describe what the author is saying or his or her point of view.

A Scribe Describes!

A person who copied information was the definition of *scribe* in ancient times. Today a scribe is a writer. Tell your students they are scribes and their job is to describe what is going on in the text they are reading. Take a few sheets of paper and tape them together lengthwise. Using scissors, make the outer edges jagged, roll it up like a scroll, and hand one to each student as you explain the role of a scribe. Feather pens are fun for this activity if you can get your hands on some. (Amazon.com has them available at various prices.) This is a wonderful learning center activity!

♦ Review Game #1: Definition Dash

After a few weeks of teaching several of the words, try a review game to help students get the information into long-term memory. This one is a favorite of mine. It provides a lot of movement, repetition, and fun!

For this review, have students bring their chairs and form a tight circle. This can be done in small groups, but I find this game in a large group is lots of fun. It begins with the teacher standing in the middle of the circle, with the students in their chairs surrounding her or him. There are no empty seats in the circle.

The teacher begins by saying something like, "I know what the definition of *analyze* is. Who else knows?" At this point students who know the definition get out of their seats and try to sit in a seat that has been left unoccupied by another student. At the same time, the teacher heads toward a seat, so one student is left in the middle. That student in the middle must give the definition of the word *analyze*. Applause follows a correct definition. Please, don't let a wrong definition go unnoticed. We don't want students to store misinformation in long-term memory. After providing the definition, the student has the opportunity to ask for the definition of another word or may ask any of the following:

"I know a synonym for *analyze*. Who else knows?"

"I know the *analyze* jingle. Who else does?"

"I can make up a sentence using *analyze*. Who else can?"

"I can draw a picture of what *analyze* means. Who else can?"

Any way that the words can be reinforced makes for a great review and encourages the brain to recall and restore the words and definitions.

The bonus to this game is that the students get in a lot of movement. If you are a student of the brain, you know that this causes the release of the chemical dopamine, which makes students feel good about the learning. The brain loves dopamine and will want to repeat activities that cause its release (Ratey, 2008). Learning, movement, and dopamine are a great memory combination!

Note: Keep track of students who do not participate and make a point to find out why. Do they not know the words and their definitions? Do they not want to speak in front of class for fear of making a mistake? If the second answer is yes, what can you do to make this a safe game so your students will not be afraid of making mistakes?

Perhaps you could make a mistake yourself. Be sure you end up in the middle and come up with an incorrect answer because you were thinking of the wrong word or forgot the question. Laugh at yourself and make it easy for your students to laugh at you. Then take the opportunity to talk about mistakes and how the brain learns from those mistakes!

Determine

Definition: conclude, decide, choose

Examples:
- Determine the meaning of a word.
- Determine the main idea.

🎵 **Jingle:**   Determine and you will find
That you have made up your mind!

Determine in the Common Core

The critical word *determine* is found in numerous standards in the CCSS beginning in 1st grade. Students will find this word throughout reading and assessments in standards for literature and in informational text. They will be expected to determine the meanings of words, phrases, and metaphors. Assessments may ask them to determine the main idea and supporting details as well as the author's point of view. It is critical for our students to recognize the word *determine* and know its meaning without a second thought so they will have the time and memory space to perform the task that is expected of them.

Determine in Webb

In Webb's Depth of Knowledge levels, determining the author's purpose, for example, is a Level 3 activity. This level is about strategic thinking, a higher-level skill, to be sure!

Concept Map

Figure 3.15 is a concept map for the word *determine*.

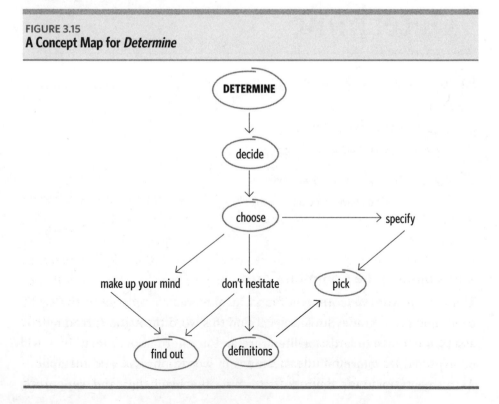

FIGURE 3.15
A Concept Map for *Determine*

Vocabulary Word Map

Figure 3.16 is a vocabulary word map for the word *determine*.

FIGURE 3.16
Vocabulary Word Map for *Determine*

Write the word.	determine
Write a definition of the word	choose
Write a synonym.	decide
Write an antonym.	can't decide
Write the word here, in color.	
Use the word in a sentence that shows its meaning.	In order to determine the meaning of the word, Chad had to choose between two possible definitions.
Draw a picture showing the meaning of the word.	

Graphic Organizer:
What Do I Know About the Word *Determine*?

For this activity, draw a rectangle and ask students to do the same. Divide the rectangle into four quadrants. In the first quadrant (upper left), write "Determine." In the second quadrant (upper right), draw a picture or other symbolic representation of the word. In the third quadrant (lower left), write "What does it mean?" In the last quadrant, write "What does it mean to me?" You may do this activity as a whole group, in small groups, or individually. For the symbolic representation I had a teacher simply write, "Eenie, meenie, miney, mo," which helped her students immediately know that determine meant to choose.

Note: If you or your students are Justin Bieber fans and you feel the lyrics are appropriate for your students, play his song "Eenie, Meenie," which provides the definition in a different, fun way: "She's indecisive, she can't decide. . ."; "You can't make up your mind, mind, mind, mind, mind. You're wasting my time, time, time, time, time."

Word Search

It is important for your students to see and recognize the critical words instantly. One way to encourage this memory association is to create a word search using ONLY the current word. In the word search in Figure 3.17, *determine* can be found six times.

As students circle the word, ask them to recite the jingle or the definition EACH TIME. You can find many word search makers online.

FIGURE 3.17
Word Search for *Determine*

Instructions: How many times can you find the word *determine*?

T	O	S	Z	E	H	U	M	R	W	E	D
D	C	N	O	N	C	R	J	M	K	Q	E
M	E	M	X	U	L	O	B	D	Q	D	T
D	E	T	E	R	M	I	N	E	V	E	E
X	F	N	E	W	J	U	R	W	L	T	R
D	E	T	E	R	M	I	N	E	O	E	M
B	O	B	P	C	M	D	H	L	Q	R	I
R	C	C	D	A	W	I	O	P	Y	M	N
S	F	T	P	K	G	L	N	U	B	I	E
D	R	N	R	S	B	S	I	E	D	N	W
P	D	E	T	E	R	M	I	N	E	E	P
M	G	S	P	K	S	L	Y	I	J	Q	O

Develop

Definition: elaborate or expand in detail

Synonyms: explain, elaborate

Examples:
- The story starts off a little slow, but as the plot continues to develop, it becomes completely captivating.
- I need to develop the main character of my narrative a little more.

♪ **Jingle:**   De-ve-lop, explain, e-la-bo-rate;
Make your writing really great!

Develop in the Common Core

In the College and Career Readiness Anchor Standards for Writing K–5, Anchor Standards 3, 4, and 5 state:

3. Write narratives to *develop* real or imagined experiences or events using effective technique, well-chosen details, and well-structured event sequences.
4. Produce clear and coherent writing in which the *development,* organization, and style are appropriate to task, purpose, and audience.
5. *Develop* and strengthen writing as needed by planning, revising, editing, rewriting, or trying a new approach.

The grade-level standards include *develop* beginning at grade 2.

Explicitly Teaching Writing Development

The process of developing good writers begins with brainstorming ideas, organizing the ideas, writing the essay, revising the essay, and proofreading the essay. This may sound boring to some students and some teachers, but it doesn't have to be that way. We can still teach writing explicitly and make it fun.

From Drawing to Writing

As Maria in *The Sound of Music* told us, "Let's start at the very beginning, a very good place to start." Before children begin to write, they draw. Once a picture is drawn, it is time to get the child to talk about it. Ask him or her to make a story about it. Ask questions to help the student fill in the blanks and to jog his or her memory.

Have students draw pictures of their personal experiences. Then have them talk about them and finally write about them.

Writing and the GRR Model

The Gradual Release of Responsibility model shifts the cognitive load from teacher to learner slowly. First, the teacher models good writing and points out the qualities of that writing. At this point, all of the responsibility is on the teacher. From here, there is a shift to shared responsibility when the students and the teacher find and point out the merits of good writing. The next step will be the students working together both finding good writing and creating good writing development. Finally, students practice and apply the skills independently (Pearson & Gallagher, 1983).

Develop a Story

To understand the meaning of the critical verb *develop*, students may need to see how a story or novel is developed. There are steps that can show them how the development works.

Most stories include a character who has a problem that he can solve. Using just these three elements, make a game out of developing a story. Take a squishy ball or some other soft item to toss to the students. Toss the ball to the first student and ask, "Who is the character?" Let that student give a very brief description like "A small boy." Then that student throws the ball to another student and asks, "What's the problem?" The student states the problem briefly: "He is lost." The next student to receive the ball is asked, "How does he solve the problem?" That student may say, "He asks for help."

The tossing can continue and other developmental questions can be asked such as "Who helped him?" "How did he get lost?" "Is he in trouble?" "Who missed him?" When the students go too far off track, stop the game and ask them to write the developed story. They can share what they write in small groups. The stories may vary!

Transforming *Develop*

Your students will see *develop* in various forms. *Development*, a noun, is included in the CCSS (as you can see in the anchor standards) and will be found in many assessments, texts, and conversations.

Distinguish

Definition: set apart, separate, tell apart, characterize, classify, categorize

♪ **Jingle:**   Distinguish from the very start.
        Decide, discriminate, and tell apart.

Example:
  • Can you distinguish between or point out differences between the two climates?

Distinguish in the Common Core

In Appendix B of the CCSS for English Language Arts and Literacy in History/Social Studies, Science, and Technical Subjects, there are several exemplars that use the verb *distinguish:*

> When discussing E. B. White's book *Charlotte's Web,* students *distinguish* their own point of view regarding Wilbur the Pig from that of Fern Arable as well as from that of the narrator. [RL.3.6]

Students determine the point of view of John Adams in his "Letter on Thomas Jefferson" and analyze how he *distinguishes* his position from an alternative approach articulated by Thomas Jefferson. [RI.7.6]

Students read two texts on the topic of pancakes (Tomie DePaola's *Pancakes for Breakfast* and Christina Rossetti's "Mix a Pancake") and *distinguish* between the text that is a storybook and the text that is a poem. [RL.K.5]

T-Chart for *Distinguish*

This lesson teaches character building as well as the word *distinguish*:

Can you distinguish between right and wrong? In the story *Pinocchio*, in order to become a "real boy," Pinocchio must learn to distinguish the difference between right and wrong. Jiminy Cricket, the character used to show Pinocchio what is right, tries to guide him to make appropriate choices. Characters in the real world try to get Pinocchio to make wrong choices. After reading the story aloud to your students, fill out a T-chart together to distinguish between right and wrong.

On the right side of the chart under the heading "Right," you might brainstorm one idea: "going to school." On the left side of the chart under "Wrong," you and your students might put "becoming an actor." Let the students discuss how they distinguish between the two with facts from the story. Have the students continue working on their charts. Be certain to continue using the word *distinguish* in the lesson.

Concept Map for *Distinguish*

Graphic organizers are so helpful for many of our students, especially those at risk. Figure 3.18 is a concept map of the word *distinguish*.

Cubing: Another 3-D Graphic Organizer

Many of you may have used the strategy called cubing to differentiate instruction in your classroom. This strategy allows students to explore a word from

FIGURE 3.18
Concept Map for the Word *Distinguish*

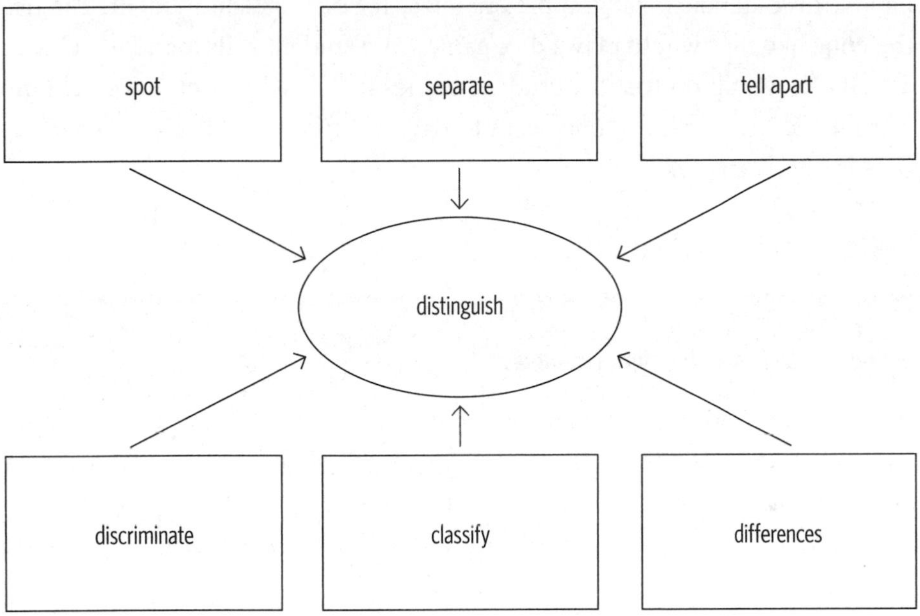

| spot | separate | tell apart |

distinguish

| discriminate | classify | differences |

six different points of view. When using a cube for a single vocabulary word, students can explore the word from these six concepts:

1. Definition of the word
2. Synonyms for the word
3. Antonyms of the word
4. Use the word in a sentence
5. Act out the word
6. Apply the word

Using the cubing template found in the appendix, you or your students cut out the cube, determine what is going to go on each of the six sides, and write the information on each. If you determine that the six concepts listed here are what you need for the word *distinguish*, the cube would look like Figure 3.19.

When the cube has all six sides filled in, it is folded and glued. You now have a three-dimensional graphic organizer for distinguish. Students can use the cube like they would play a dice game. One student rolls it and whichever activity shows up on top, the student carries it out. When you have recently introduced the word, you may want to have all students in the group participate in each activity.

FIGURE 3.19
A Cube for Studying the Word *Distinguish*

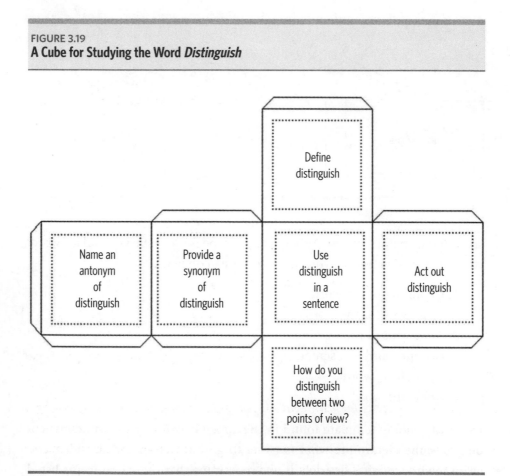

Draw

Definition: take or pull out

♪ **Jingle:**   Draw—point it out, take it out, pull it out—Draw!

Synonyms: formulate*, pull

Antonyms: put in, shorten

Example:

- The students had to draw their own conclusions about the outcome of the novel *The Giver* by Lois Lowry.

Draw in Webb's DOK

Having the ability to draw conclusions or draw inferences is a strategic thinking skill, according to Webb's Depth of Knowledge, which puts this word at Level 3.

Draw in the Common Core

In the CCSS, we see a form of the word *draw* beginning with 1st grade. First grade standard 5 in the Reading Standards for Literature K–5 states:

> RL.1.5. Explain major differences between books that tell stories and books that give information, *drawing* on a wide reading of a range of text types.

Appendix B of the CCSS uses a form of *draw* in Sample Performance Tasks for Stories and Poetry:

> Students (*with prompting and support from the teacher*) when listening to Laura Ingalls Wilder's *Little House in the Big Woods* ask questions about the events that occur (such as the encounter with the bear) and answer by offering key details *drawn* from the text. [RL.1.1]

As illustrated in these examples, it is important that you take special care and time to teach students how *draw* can be transformed. You will also have to discuss how the word *draw* has multiple meanings. Most students will automatically think that *draw, drawn,* and *drawing* have to do with creating pictures. This may be a good time to use the critical verbs *compare* and *contrast* as you examine the multiple meanings.

Transform *Draw*

Students will encounter variations of the word *draw*, such as *drawing* and *drawn*. Take some time to cover these transformations.

Web Graphic Organizer

For the word *draw*, I chose a web type of graphic organizer. You may want to show your students the multiple meanings of the word *draw,* so I created two webs and connected them (see Figure 3.20).

FIGURE 3.20
Two Webs for Multiple Definitions of the Word *Draw*

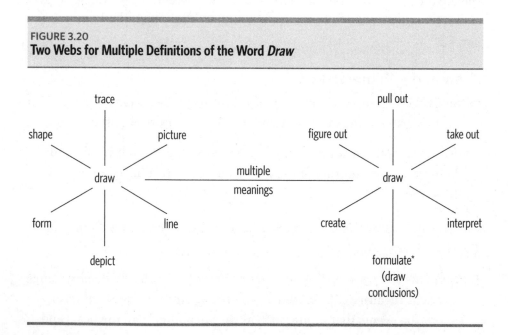

Ready? Okay!

Being a cheerleading coach for several years made me realize the power of movement and rhythm when it comes to memory. Both cheerleaders and those who want to be cheerleaders are usually willing and anxious to perform. Using the jingle or making up their own words, students create a cheer for any of the critical verbs. They can teach the others if they are interested. Many of our students need movement to help them remember. A cheer allows students to store the information in nonmotor and motor procedural memory.

Say the "Secret" Word

This activity is similar to "Who Am I?" except students know the word they have. Write the vocabulary words on the front of index cards and a simple definition on the back, or have the students create them. Tell the students that it is their duty to teach their word to every student in the class, and it is also their job to learn the other students' words.

Evaluate

Definition: find value, judge, appraise

Synonyms: weigh, estimate, gauge, calculate

🎵 **Jingle:**   I evaluate cuz I'm the judge.
                 I critique without a grudge!

Movement: Pound a fist on the palm of the other hand as though it is a gavel.

Example:

- My teacher will evaluate my paper and give me suggestions to improve my writing.

Evaluate in the Common Core

The CCSS Anchor Standards for Reading under Integration of Knowledge and Ideas include the following:

7. Integrate and *evaluate* content presented in diverse media and formats, including visually and quantitatively, as well as in words.
8. Delineate and *evaluate* the argument and specific claims in a text, including the validity of the reasoning as well as the relevance and sufficiency of the evidence.

The Anchor Standards for Speaking and Listening include these:

2. Integrate and *evaluate* information presented in diverse media and formats, including visually, quantitatively, and orally.
3. *Evaluate* a speaker's point of view, reasoning, and use of evidence and rhetoric.

In Appendix B of the CCSS, there are exemplars such as the following:

Students *evaluate* Jim Murphy's *The Great Fire* to identify which aspects of the text (e.g., loaded language and the inclusion of particular facts) reveal his purpose, presenting Chicago as a city that was "ready to burn." [RH.6–8.6]

Evaluate in Bloom

The ability to evaluate is one of the highest levels of thinking, according to Bloom's revised taxonomy (Anderson & Krathwohl, 2001). Evaluating includes the ability to hypothesize, critique, experiment, judge, test, detect, and monitor.

Nonlinguistic Representation: A Picture!

Nonlinguistic representations do not have to be pictures. However experts such as Ruby Payne (2009) say kids (especially kids from low-income families) who can't draw it don't know it, so I encourage pictures with most vocabulary words. For the word *evaluate* many students draw a judge sitting on his bench pounding his gavel. It is a good reminder of the definition.

A teacher in one of my workshops shared an idea that reinforced the critical words and decorated her room as well. She assigned each of her 30 students one of the critical words. Their assignment was to create a poster for the room with a picture and a sentence explaining the meaning of the word. Not all of her students were comfortable with drawing, so they were allowed to find appropriate pictures on the Internet or in magazines to paste on their posters. Students knowing these words will benefit all classes, so other faculty were recruited to assist students in this undertaking. The ideas had to come from the students themselves, but help with pictures and symbols from others were allowed. The posters were all made on 12 × 18 inch paper, which made it easier to place them around the room. Some teachers said they would put no such parameters on the posters as they wanted the students to formulate their own plan.

Evaluation Lesson

Some students don't understand how to evaluate or judge. (If you have previously taught them the word *support*, it might be easier.) This is another opportunity to use technology. You want them to have something to evaluate. A website might be motivating, but any other text will do.

1. Find a website that is appropriate for your grade level. All students will be evaluating the same material. Tell them that they are to evaluate what they see and read. They are judges!
2. Ask them to look at the site or material carefully and jot down a few notes. Give them a few leading questions such as "What do you think of this website? Do you think someone your age would be attracted to it? Do you think you could learn something from this site?"
3. After working alone, students find a partner, or assign partners. Have them compare notes. What differences do they find in their notes? What did one person notice that the other did not?
4. Form larger groups and give them time to follow the same process. See if they can come to some consensus on the value of the material. Do they see strengths and weaknesses?
5. Give each group the opportunity to give one statement or judgment that they agree upon. Do they have support for their statements? What is it? Write these on the board for all to see.

6. After you have developed this list, ask students what they did to evaluate. Did they follow a system or model? Could this be useful when asked to evaluate something else?

Explain

Definition: tell about something so people understand it

Synonyms: clarify, demonstrate, interpret, describe in detail, define

Examples:

- Explain how an author uses reasons and evidence to support particular points in a text.
- Explain major differences between . . .
- Explain how a text's illustrations . . .
- What is the author trying to explain in this text?
- Scientists could not explain the strange lights in the sky.
- I don't know how to explain the dog's strange behavior.
- We asked him to explain his reasons to us.

♫ **Jingle:**   Explain! Explain!
And always make it plain!

Explain in the Common Core

The word *explain* is found in the CCSS beginning in 1st grade.

In the CCSS under Reading Standards for Literature K–5:

10. *Explain* major differences between books that tell stories and books that give information, drawing on a wide reading of a range of text types.

Slap the Word!

Put students in small groups and pass out a set of cards with the critical words they have learned thus far written on them. Each group has the same words, but it may be easier to keep the sets separate if they are printed on different-colored paper. Call out a word and the first player to slap the card with the word on it gets to keep it. The student with the most cards at the end wins the game.

Frayer Model

Using the template in the appendix at the end of the book, have students fill in the four quadrants.

What It Says/What It Means T-Chart

The following chart is useful to get students started on the road to explain in a plain and simple manner. Provide some short text to begin getting students to do closer reading. College and Career Readiness Anchor Standards for Reading (National Governors Association, 2010) list Standard 1 for both K–5 and 6–12 under Key Ideas and Details:

1. Read closely to determine what the text says explicitly and to make logical inferences from it; cite specific textual evidence when writing or speaking to support conclusions drawn from the text.

Using a T-chart, students write what the text says (the main points) on the left and explain what it means on the right.

"Read Like a Reporter and Write Like a Detective"

David Coleman (2011) makes the statement in this heading about the CCSS. We want our students to read closely and write proficiently.

Ask, "What does a detective do that can be compared to a reader engaging with text?" Ask your students to read text closely. Begin with short passages and teach them to annotate the text. (This includes "taking notes" by circling words they are unsure of, underlining what they don't understand, putting stars by key ideas and important details, and/or jotting down a summary in the margins as they read.) As they learn to do this and you discuss the text with them, they will learn what is important to explain. Of course, this strategy will work for other critical words such as *describe, delineate,* and *determine.*

Read with a Pencil

Having students read with a pencil in hand helps them read closely, understand or ask questions so they will understand, and underline or highlight important points. Using sticky notes is another option for this kind of reading. Close reading is suggested by the Common Core reading standards, so as you teach your students the word *explain,* you can show them how reading and highlighting or using sticky notes will help them find what they will need to explain.

Identify

Definition: isolate, point out, find, discover, cite*

Synonyms: point, find, discover

🎵 **Jingle:** Identify is to detect
                information from the text!

Movement: Place the pointer finger of one hand on the nose. Take the other pointer finger and act like you are pointing to something.

Identify in the Common Core

The critical verb *identify* is found throughout the English Language Arts and Literacy in History/Social Studies, Science, and Technical Subjects standards.

In Appendix B of the CCSS, exemplars such as the following are found:

1. Students *identify* <u>the points</u> at which different characters are telling the story in the "Finn Family Moomintroll" by Tove Jansson. [RL.1.6]
2. Students *identify* <u>the reasons</u> Clyde Robert Bulla gives in his book *A Tree Is a Plant* in support of his point about the function of roots in germination. [RI.1.8]
3. Students read Paul Fleischman's poem "Fireflies," determining the meaning of words and phrases in the poem, particularly focusing on <u>*identifying* his use of nonliteral language</u> and talking about how it suggests meaning. [RL.3.4]

Here is an example of the Reading Standards for Literature K–5 from kindergarten:

2. With prompting and support, *identify* characters, settings, and major events in a story.

Identify in Webb

Identify can be found in three of the four levels of Webb's Depth of Knowledge. Students need to be able to identify major events or details in a narrative, and identify research questions and design investigations for a scientific problem (Webb, 2005).

Consider the following two sentences and compare the depth of thought and skill for each:

1. Identify the main character in the story.
2. Identify the source of the information given in the passage.

Concept Map for *Identify*

I think it is prudent to use some type of graphic organizer for the critical words. Figure 3.21 is a concept map for *identify.*

Which One of These Doesn't Belong?

Sesame Street and other children's shows have the right idea with segments like, "One of these things is not like the others." This is a great game to play with students learning vocabulary.

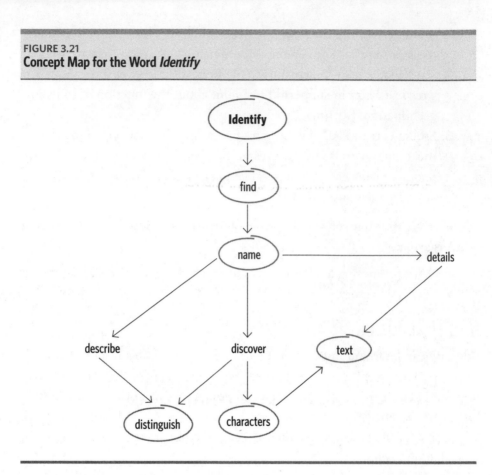

FIGURE 3.21
Concept Map for the Word *Identify*

As students enter the room, have four words in plain sight (on the board, bulletin board, projector screen, etc.). After they are seated, ask them, "Which of these words doesn't belong?" When you have agreed on the odd word, discuss what the others have in common and what separates the word that doesn't belong from the others.

Example
- Identify
- Distinguish

- Cite
- Evaluate

  Evaluate is the odd word. Have students discuss how *identify, distinguish,* and *cite* are alike and different.

Flash Cards

Getting information into nonmotor procedural memory (automatic) can be attained by using flash cards. The act of the response becoming automatic tells you that the goal is being reached. Have students make flash cards of any of the words with which they have difficulty. You may wish to make flash cards for every word for some students.

For some students, the critical word on one side and a short definition on the other side will suffice. Others may benefit from having both the definition and a picture on the side opposite the word itself.

What Critical Word Am I?

This is sometimes an icebreaker at parties. When you arrive at the party, the host puts the name of a famous person on your back. You walk around the room introducing yourself (your real name) and then ask yes or no questions of your new acquaintance to help you deduce whose name is on your back. In the classroom, you use the critical vocabulary words. Write the words on index cards and tape them to the backs of the students. Have them walk around and ask questions until they figure out which word is on their back.

You can go beyond yes or no questions if you wish to challenge both students. A student can ask another student to look at the word on her back and ask for an example—without using the word—and that keeps all students thinking and remembering the words they have stored in their brains.

For instance, Devon has the word *compare* on his back. Cheryl may give him the following example or clue: "I read the text and found that Max and Lucy had a lot of things in common."

Review Game #2: Bingo

Hand out bingo cards with definitions written in the squares. Have students walk around the room asking their classmates if they know what word fits the definition in a square. If the student knows, he or she signs his or her name in that square. After all the squares are filled with signatures, everyone sits down. You then, pull names out of a container and call them out. If a student has that person's signature on his or her card, he or she gets to cover up the space. Rick Wormeli (2005) suggests using M&M's or popcorn. The first student to get five in a row yells, "Bingo." Have the student read each square's definition and the name of the student who signed the square. That student must say the word that matches the definition. If all five of the students know the definitions, the game is over and everyone gets to have a good time eating their bingo markers.

Infer

Definition: deduce; conclude; use information to make educated guesses based on prior knowledge.

♪ **Jingle:**   Infer! Read between the lines.
              See what info you can find.

Movement: Put fingers horizontally in front of the eyes.

Text + What I Know = Infer (inference)

Example of a conversation in which you must infer to understand:

"You do it."
"No. You ."
"I'm not doing it."
"You're older."
"She won't even know it's gone."

"Yes, she will."

"Not 'til tomorrow."

"Yeah, but she can't go to school with just one!"

"They're way too big".

"But what will we use for Cinderella?"

"Maybe she can leave something else behind."

Who is speaking?

What are they talking about doing?

What do we know about the story?

<u>Observe and see what is there</u>

<u>Infer and find out what is not there</u>

I can infer from his actions that he is going to miss school.

Knowing the word *infer* and then the noun, *inference,* is a huge step into higher-level thinking. Many students know how to infer, but they don't know what they are doing. Sounds weird, but if we ask students a question like "From the following reading, what can you conclude?" they can give the inference but don't know that is what it is called.

Craigslist posting:

Please help me find Spooky. She is black and has one white paw. Spooky is wearing a purple collar, and when you pet her she will purr. Call 555-5555 if you see her. The last time I saw her, she was on my corner.

What Is Spooky?

Where might we find Spooky?

Bagging It!

Bring a variety of items in a bag or box. Tell the students these are props for a play. As you bring out each item, discuss what it is and who would use it.

Possible bag items: flashlight, thermometer, screwdriver, legal pad, spatula, stopwatch, gardening gloves, journal.

Sherlock Holmes

Explain to students that Sherlock Holmes was a famous fictional detective. From the discussion, be certain each student knows what a detective is. Perhaps they have read *Encyclopedia Brown, Boy Detective.* Talk about what detectives do. After students determine that detectives find clues and figure out mysteries, give students a list of clues. In groups, tell them that they are to be detectives and infer what they can from the information.

KIS Strategy

KIS stands for Key words, Infer, Support.

This mnemonic strategy helps students remember the three steps in making and supporting inferences.

Students need to underline <u>key</u> words and facts from the text.

Next students make <u>inferences</u> using the key words or facts to answer the question.

Lastly, the students list background knowledge used to <u>support</u> their answers.

While teaching middle and high school, I loved to use the short story "The Lady or the Tiger" to teach my students inference.

Integrate

Definition: put together, combine

Synonyms: unify, unite, mix

♫ **Jingle:**   Integrate and unite,
                Make sure things fit just right!

Movement: Fold hands.

Integrate in the Common Core

In the Common Core Anchor Standards for Reading, Standard 7 under Integration of Knowledge and Ideas states:

> 7. *Integrate* and evaluate content presented in diverse media and formats, including visually and quantitatively, as well as in words.

Because the standards suggest that students read multiple texts in multiple genres and media, it will be necessary for them to integrate what they read to make sense of it for themselves and for the audience they address.

Freeze Frame

Integrate is a great word for this game. Put students in small groups and have them come up with an idea for becoming statues that express the idea of integrate or integration. For instance, they could huddle together in a small circle leaving a space for one person outside the group. The two people on either side of the opening can have their hands out as though they are encouraging or inviting the outsider into the circle.

An Emotional Hook

With older students, you may talk about integration from a historical perspective. In U.S. history, integration was the goal of an organized movement to break down the barriers of discrimination and segregation separating African Americans from the rest of American society. A brainstorming session or group discussions may bring up some strong feelings about the injustice of segregation. Through this discussion you can begin looking at the various definitions of *integrate* and have the students create their definition of *integrate* according to the standards.

Apple Pie and Baseball

The word *integrate* can be used with two of America's famous icons. Making apple pie includes being able to integrate—combine—several ingredients. In particular, younger students may relate to using this metaphor, although older students and adults can use this example as a mental picture of the meaning of *integrate*. You can talk about baking in general, and include recipes that call for mixing ingredients together.

Baseball historically has represented much of what has happened in our country. The process of immigrants coming to America and being widely accepted into our favorite pastime has been shared in articles and books. For more information on the history of baseball and how it began to integrate various ethnicities into the leagues, visit *History Today* online at http://www.historytoday.com/william-rubinstein/jackie-robinson-and-integration-major-league-baseball.

Mind Map

Figure 3.22 shows one way to mind-map the word *integrate*. If your students can do this on their own, coming up with their own words, symbols, and connections, that is best. If not, this will provide you with some ideas to help them.

FIGURE 3.22
Mind Map of the Word *Integrate*

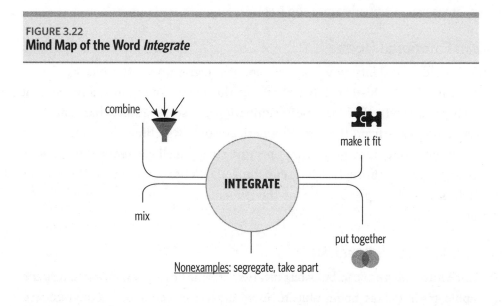

Interpret

Definition: describe what you have found out

Synonyms: translate, decode, explain*, clarify

♪ **Jingle:**   Interpret and explain.
          Make things clear and you will gain!

Interpret in Webb and Bloom

Interpret is listed as a Level 2 word in Webb's Depth of Knowledge, as it is considered a skill or concept that students learn. Bloom's new taxonomy (Anderson & Krathwohl, 2001) shows *interpret* at the lower level of Understanding.

Interpret in the Common Core

College and Career Readiness Anchor Standards for Reading, Anchor Standard 4 states:

> 4. *Interpret* words and phrases as they are used in a text, including determining technical, connotative, and figurative meanings, and analyze how specific word choices shape meaning or tone.

Reading Standards for Informational Text in grade 4 includes:

> RI.4.7. *Interpret* information presented visually, orally, or quantitatively (e.g., in charts, graphs, diagrams, time lines, animations, or interactive elements on Web pages) and explain how the information contributes to an understanding of the text in which it appears.

Although the CCSS does not include the word *interpret* until grade 4, the skill of interpretation begins even before kindergarten. Children must be able to interpret the following:

- Gestures and facial expressions
- Directions that they are given
- Stories that they hear
- Stories that they read
- Important data that may affect them

Appendix B Sample Performance Task for Informational Texts:

Students *interpret* the visual chart that accompanies Steve Otfinoski's *The Kid's Guide to Money: Earning It, Saving It, Spending It, Growing It, Sharing It* and explain how the information found within it contributes to an understanding of how to create a budget. [RI.4.7]

Vocabulary Gloves

Create vocabulary gloves for *interpret*. Here are some ideas:

Palm: Sentence
How should we interpret her behavior?

Thumb: Definition
explain

Index finger: synonym
decode

Middle finger: synonym
make clear or clarify

Ring finger: synonym
shed light on

Pinky: antonym
misinterpret

What Do You See?

Many teachers find that beginning to teach students to interpret using pictures is a good way to start. Before they interpret what they hear or what they read, have them look closely at some pictures. Norman Rockwell's wonderful

Saturday Evening Post magazine covers lead to much interpretation. You may be able to find magazine copies or prints of his pictures available at libraries. You, your colleagues, or your students may even have a print at home.

For instance, Rockwell's picture entitled "Oh, Yeah" is one that students enjoy discussing. The picture depicts boys in basketball uniforms in a circle arguing about basketball. A ball is in one boy's hand. The question to ask your students is "How would you interpret this picture?"

Word Wall Bingo

If you have a word wall of the critical words in your classroom, word wall bingo is a fun way to interact with your wall. Have students make a large tic-tac-toe grid on a piece of paper. Then they look at the word wall and fill in each space on the grid with a word. Randomly call out nine words from the wall. The first student who covers all nine spaces on the grid is the winner. You can then debrief the activity by talking about the definitions of the words. A variation is to say definitions of the words and see if students know the words well enough to cover them.

Locate

Definition: find

Synonyms: find, trace, discover, uncover

Antonyms: lose, miss, misplace

🎵 **Jingle:**   Locate and uncover
New things you discover

Movement: Have students touch their chest, front pockets of their pants (act as though they have pants with pockets, and their back pockets as though they are looking for something they may have on them. (Think of a man checking for his wallet or glasses.)

Examples

- I thought I had lost my new scarf, but I was able to locate it in my bottom drawer.
- The question at the end of the chapter asked me to locate details that would support the lady choosing the tiger in "The Lady or the Tiger."
- I located the supporting facts easily.

Locate in Bloom

Although the critical verb *locate* is sometimes considered to be in the lowest level of Bloom's taxonomy, Knowledge or Remember (depending on whether you are using the "old" Bloom [1956] or the "new" Bloom [Anderson & Krathwohl, 2001]), it is also considered to be at the Comprehension level. This level requires students to grasp the meaning of information rather than just restate it.

Locate in the Common Core

In Appendix B of the CCSS for English Language Arts/Literacy, *locate* is found in several of the possible examples of assessment questions. Below is one of them.

> Students *locate* key facts or information in Claire Llewellyn's *Earthworms* by using various text features (headings, table of contents, glossary) found in the text. [RI.1.5]

Draw a Picture

Ask students to draw a picture demonstrating their understanding of the word *locate.*

Some students draw stick figures of a person happily showing something in their hand and shouting, "I found it! I was able to locate it!"

Location! Location! Location!

After a brief discussion of the word *locate* (which may include questioning such as "When have you had to locate something? What did you have to locate? Were you always able to locate what you needed to find?"), tell students that you are going to ask them to locate things in the school or in the classroom. In scavenger hunt style, put students in groups and give them a list of what they have to locate. On the sheet of paper you give them, have a column in which they can write the location of what they have located. One of the items may be the word *locate,* which may be located anywhere, even on your critical word wall. Students will enjoy the movement, be motivated by the competition, and will repeatedly repeat the word *locate* as each item on your list should begin with the verb *locate.*

Your list may include these items:

- Locate the word *locate.*
- Locate three books by Judy Blume (write the names of the books and the location).
- Locate the school newsletter on the school's website.
- Locate the teacher's edition of your math book.
- Locate the principal.
- Locate something in your pocket.
- Locate the key facts from last night's reading.

Which One Doesn't Belong?

In the section on *identify,* I suggested you could play "Which of These Words Doesn't Belong?" with four words. The game would be appropriate for *locate* as well.

Example:

- Describe
- Locate
- Summarize
- Paraphrase

Locate does not belong. *Describe* means to show details, *summarize* to sum up the entire reading, and *paraphrase* asks the reader to put the selection in his or her own words. *Locate* asks the reader to find some specific information.

Transform *Locate*

Add suffixes and prefixes to locate to create new words like *location, locating, located,* and *relocate.* Ask students to work in small groups and discuss the meanings of these words. Have the students write sentences using these words and others they may know. For instance, one of my students said, "I dislocated my shoulder once." This brought about great discussion of the transformed verb.

Organize

Definition: arrange, classify, order, consolidate, unify

Synonyms: sort out, systematize, planned

♫ **Jingle:**　　Organize, arrange, get it done!
　　　　　　　　This makes time to have more fun!

Organize in the Common Core

This critical verb presents itself under various standards and grade levels. You will find it in the Writing Standards K–5, Speaking and Listening Standards K–5, Reading Standards for Informational Text 6–12, Writing Standards 6–12, and Writing Standards for Literacy in History/Social Studies, Science, and Technical Subjects 6–12. It begins at grade 3 with the writing standard 3.a:

> 3.a. Establish a situation and introduce a narrator and/or characters; *organize* an event sequence that unfolds naturally.

The Speaking and Listening Standards at grade 4 state:

> 4. Report on a topic or text, tell a story, or recount an experience in an *organized* manner, using appropriate facts and relevant, descriptive details to support main ideas or themes; speak clearly at an understandable pace.

Try It!

Students often have trouble organizing information in their writing. Learning this word is an opening for you to assign students to write an organized paragraph, essay, or story in which they use 5 to 10 of the critical verbs.

Understanding *Organize*

Mrs. Blundy begins the school year showing her classes two student desks that she has set up as a display. One desk is organized: notebook on the left side, extra paper on top of the notebook, spiral notebooks on top of those, and two folders top off that side. On the right side of the desk she displays a pouch of pencils, pens, a protractor, and a ruler. Beneath the pouch is the homework folder (papers to be "left" at home in the left pouch, papers to be brought "right" back to school on the right). There are different colored folders for each subject area that are neatly labeled. Students have not received their textbooks yet, so they will be placed in a proper order when they are handed out. The disorganized desk is a disaster. Paper falls out the moment she tries to remove anything. Pencils roll on the floor. The folders are in the desk in various positions with papers hanging out of them. Mrs. Blundy asks one child to sit at each desk. She takes out a stopwatch and announces that they are going to have a contest to see how long it takes each student to get items out of the desks. She begins by asking the students to find an eraser, then a reading folder, and finally a black spiral notebook. It is clear that the organized desk makes it much easier to find items. Organization is the clear winner!

Mrs. Blundy then explains that an organized desk allows the students to have a more organized mind. She shares scenarios like this:

> When I ask Disorganized Dan to take out his reading folder and begin writing a paragraph that compares and contrasts the two characters in the short story they are reading, by the time Dan finds his folder and a pencil with which to write, he has forgotten the assignment! His working memory did not have enough space to hold onto the assignment. It was too busy wondering what he was grabbing from the desk and worrying that he would never find what he

needed. Worry can take up memory space, too. Organized Ophelia, in contrast, gets her supplies out of her desk in seconds and begins her work. She has no stress and plenty of memory space to think about her assignment.

Mrs. Blundy actually uses this lesson as the opening for another lesson: compare and contrast. What do you suppose their first compare and contrast assignment is going to be? Compare and contrast an organized desk with a disorganized desk.

Transforming *Organize*

Students will encounter various forms of the word *organize*. Take time to review these transformations: *organized, organization,* and *organizing.*

Synonym Wheel

Organize has many synonyms. Knowing those synonyms may help students understand and cement the word in their long-term memory. Figure 3.23

FIGURE 3.23
Synonym Wheel for *Organize*

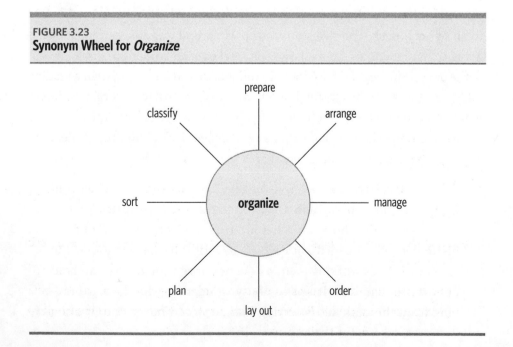

shows a sample of a synonym wheel for *organize*. In the appendix you will find a blank wheel, so your students can fill it in with the words they choose. The act of thinking about the word and creating the wheel themselves may assist with memory.

Refer

Definition: mention or direct for information

Synonyms: name, cite*, talk about, bring up, describe*, signify, represent, relate, indicate, suggest*

♫ **Jingle:**   Refer is to mention
Information for attention.

Keyword Mnemonic: This strategy is similar to a play on words. Use a word that is similar to the critical word to help students relate to the word and remember it.

"I *prefer* that you refer to your reading materials for proof to support your answer."

Refer in the Common Core

Under Reading Standards for Literature K–5 are the first grade-level standards for grades 3 and 4:

RL.3.1. Ask and answer questions to demonstrate understanding of a text, *referring* explicitly to the text as the basis for the answers.

RL.4.1. *Refer* to details and examples in a text when explaining what the text says explicitly and when drawing inferences from the text.

Sample Performance Tasks for Stories and Poetry in Appendix B of the ELA Standards

- Students ask and answer questions regarding the plot of Patricia MacLachlan's *Sarah, Plain and Tall*, explicitly *referring* to the book to form the basis for their answers. [RL.3.1]

- Students explain the selfish behavior by Mary and make inferences regarding the impact of the cholera outbreak in Frances Hodgson Burnett's *The Secret Garden* by explicitly *referring to* details and examples from the text. [RL.4.1]
- Students *refer* to the structural elements (e.g., verse, rhythm, meter) of Ernest Lawrence Thayer's "Casey at the Bat" when analyzing the poem and contrasting the impact and differences of those elements to a prose summary of the poem. [RL.4.5]

Transforming *Refer*

Students should become familiar with *referred*, *referring*, and *reference* as you teach the word *refer*. They will come across these words on assessments, in conversations, and in text.

Sample sentences:

- I referred to the detail in Chapter 6 to prove my point.
- My doctor will refer me to a specialist.
- I will refer to details in the text to support my reason for believing Tim is innocent.
- When the principal walked in and said, "Come to the office," I was not sure to whom she was referring.

Use It or They Will Lose It

Refer is a word that can easily be inserted into conversation and teaching lessons. Start using *refer* in class. Here are some suggestions:

- "I refer you to page 7 in your text."
- "I will refer to the poem we read last night."
- "In comparing the two readings, I will refer to each one as I compare them."

Who Has It?

With the students in groups, hand out a set of index cards that are set up like this: On the front of the first card it says "I have *refer*." On the back it has a definition like "Who has a word that means_____?" The person with that word reads it and then turns the card over and it says, "Who has a word that means_____."

🧩 Review Game #3: Game Show

This game has become one of my favorites to share with teachers at conferences and workshops. I originally learned this one from Debra Pickering, author of many educational books such as *Classroom Instruction That Works* (Marzano, Pollack, & Pickering, 2001). This game is along the lines of the old television show *Password* with a bit of *$10,000 Pyramid* mixed in. Students are asked to pair up, with one student facing the screen, whiteboard, or any area where you might be able to display a list of words without the students seeing them until you are ready. I put this game on a PowerPoint slide for my workshops.

The slide contains a list of the critical words that have been taught. This is not a pre-assessment tool—it is best to use this as a review. The student facing the screen is the clue giver. Once all the students are assembled properly so that the student giving the answers cannot see the screen, I reveal the list of words.

The clue giver provides the definition or examples until the partner says the word. They may skip a word and come back to it. When we first play the game, it is not over until everyone has been successful. As the students become more comfortable with the game, I may make it more competitive and give a small token for being done first. I may give the winning team a sticker, a pencil, or a small privilege. This game does not require a reward as most students love playing.

I find the novelty does not wear off quickly, if at all, as long as I don't play the game more than once a week. This is a great game for getting these words and definitions into long-term memory. Keep in mind that the clue giver has to know the definitions and examples to keep the partnership successful. When we have learned at least 10 words, I have two screens of words and have the partners trade places.

Retell

Defintion: tell in your own words; tell again in your own way

Synonyms: repeat, restate, recap, relate again or differently, summarize*, paraphrase*, cite*

🎵 **Jingle:**   Retell means to repeat or recite;
                  Tell it again and do it right!

Movement: Students hold their hand up to their ear as though they are talking on the phone. Say the first line of the jingle with the left hand and the second with the right.

Example:
* I like to listen to my uncle retell his stories from his trip to Alaska.

Retell in the Common Core

The retelling of narrative and expository text has been shown to enhance comprehension (DeTemple & Tabors, 1996). The CCSS asks for more informational text, as well as the reading of multiple complex texts of different genres with an understanding of the differences in point of view, the genres themselves, and the key ideas.

In Appendix B of the CCSS there are exemplars such as the following:

Students *retell* Arnold Lobel's *Frog and Toad Together* while demonstrating their understanding of a central message or lesson of the story (e.g., how friends are able to solve problems together or how hard work pays off). [RL.1.2]

In the CCSS Reading Standards for Literature at the kindergarten level, Standard 2 reads:

RL.K.2. With prompting and support, *retell* familiar stories, including key details.

In the Reading Standards for Informational Text, Standard 2 states:

RI.K.2. With prompting and support, identify the main topic and *retell* key details of a text.

Students are asked to retell what they read both verbally and in writing beginning in kindergarten. Yet when I ask beginning 1st graders to retell what I read, they don't understand what I am asking, even though I have seen the word *retell* used on some of their homework papers.

Retell-ephone

Do you remember playing the game Telephone as a child? This was a favorite at home and at school. I used the strategy with middle schoolers as well as kindergartners. It is fun and can be a useful tool.

In the original game, the teacher provided a statement to a student. The student was to whisper the statement to the next person, and this would continue until the last person in the room or group reported aloud what the statement was. The purpose of the game is active listening, although the difficulty in hearing the sentence often resulted in a very different rendering of the original sentence. This made the game funny and fun.

For our retell-ephone purpose, I follow these steps:

1. Students read or are read a very short passage.
2. Each student formulates his own one-sentence retelling.
3. Students are put in groups and one student is designated as the official reteller.
4. This student whispers his retell to the next until the last person in the group declares what she has heard.

Benefits of the format:

- Each student has a better idea of what the reteller is saying since they have heard or read the passage. There will be fewer dramatic changes in the sentence.
- Each student is retelling a retell, which reinforces the concept of retelling.
- When the last person retells aloud, the students can discuss the accuracy of the retell.

Transforming Retell

You can see how many different forms of *retell* that were used in the previous activity. It will be important that students understand how prefixes and suffixes change the meaning of the word and also the part of speech.

Which One Doesn't Belong?

Of the following four words, *locate* does not belong. Ask your students how *retell, paraphrase,* and *summarize* are alike and different.

1. Retell
2. Paraphrase
3. Summarize
4. Locate

Suggest

Definition: propose as fitting

Synonyms: advise, recommend, advocate, say, put forth, propose

🎵 **Jingle:**   Recommend, put forth, suggest;
Propose ideas that are the best.

Suggest in the Common Core

Reading Standard for Literature K–5

Grade 1 Standard 4:

Identify words and phrases in stories or poems that *suggest* feelings or appeal to the senses.

Appendix B Text Exemplars and Sample Performance Tasks

Students identify words and phrases within Molly Bang's *The Paper Crane* that appeal to the senses and *suggest* the feelings of happiness experienced by the owner of the restaurant (e.g., clapped, played, loved, overjoyed). [RL.1.4]

Students read Paul Fleischman's poem "Fireflies," determining the meaning of words and phrases in the poem, particularly focusing on identifying his use of nonliteral language (e.g., "light is the ink we use") and talking about how it *suggests* meaning. [RL.3.4]

Transforming *Suggest*

Suggesting, suggested, suggestion, and *suggestive* are forms of *suggest* that students will encounter in many situations.

Examples:

- Are you *suggesting* that Wilbur did not like Charlotte in *Charlotte's Web?*
- It was *suggested* that Tom Sawyer did not always do what he was told.
- The author's setting was *suggestive* of a western town.

What Do You Suggest?

Using the statement "What do you suggest?" or "What do you think the author suggests?" can be one way to get this word into long-term memory. Put students in groups, and write the question on the board or somewhere the students can see it in order to repeat it. Have one person in each group begin and ask the question with the emphasis on the first word, *what.* Moving in a clockwise fashion, the next student asks the question with an emphasis on the second word, *do.* Continue around the group until the question has been asked with emphasis on each word. (Skip the word *the* in this activity.)

You may want to write the question with the words underlined or italicized:

- <u>What</u> do you think the author suggests?
- What <u>do</u> you think the author suggests?
- What do <u>you</u> think the author suggests?
- What do you <u>think</u> the author suggests?
- What do you think the <u>author</u> suggests?
- What do you think the author <u>suggests</u>?

The purpose of this activity is to have the students hear the word repeated to help them remember it, to appreciate the slight differences when different words are emphasized, and to get them to think about what the word *suggest* suggests. Have a large-group discussion about what the word *suggest* means to each student.

Synonym Wheel

Suggest works well with a synonym wheel (see Figure 3.24).

FIGURE 3.24
Synonym Wheel for the Word *Suggest*

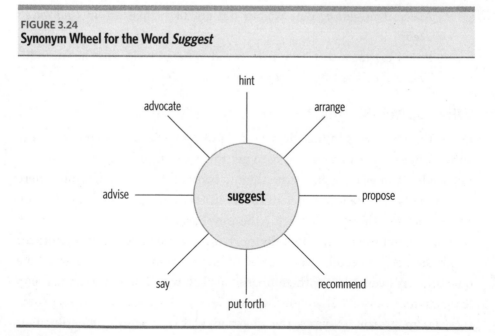

Summarize/Paraphrase

Definition: make a short statement of the main points of a passage

Synonyms: review, condense, sum up

🎵 **Jingle:**   Summarize and make it shorter;
                 Just the facts, like a reporter.

I have combined *summarize* and *paraphrase* because the words are often taught together. However, I would initially teach them one at a time, to avoid confusing students.

According to the work of Marzano et al. (2001), students had a 34 percentile gain when taught how to summarize information and take effective notes. Those students needed to know what was expected of them when they were asked to summarize. In the second edition of *Classroom Instruction That Works* (Dean, Hubbell, Pitler, & Stone, 2012), the authors suggest that students do four things to summarize: delete what's not important, remove repetitions, replace lists with single words that describe the list, and find or create a topic sentence. A common critical word on assessments and classroom assignments, we must take the time to teach our students what they need to do in order to summarize and to compare this process to paraphrasing, which is also on our critical word list.

What's It All About?

In *Classroom Instruction That Works*, 2nd edition, Dean and colleagues (2012) suggest using summary frames when you begin to teach students how to summarize. Summary frames are also available in *Summarization in Any Subject* (Wormeli, 2005). Following are a few suggestions for teaching summary frames to your students.

Narrative:

1. Who? Who is the story talking about?
2. When does the story take place? Where?
3. What started the action in the story?
4. What happened next?
5. How did the story end?

Problem-Solution

1. What is the problem?
2. What was done to solve the problem?
3. Was there a good result?

Cause-Effect

1. What happened first? (the cause)
2. What was the result? (the effect)

The questions for summarization may look simple, but most students need a way to begin to approach the text. Although our purpose is to engrain the word *summarize* into our student's nonmotor procedural memory, knowing that definition is related to something they do is helpful.

Tweet, Tweet!

If you happen to have a class in which all of the students have access to Twitter, you may want to set up a classroom Twitter account. This is a fun way to get students to summarize since Twitter only allows 140 characters per tweet. Even without the technology, you can tell students that they are going to learn to follow the Twitter format and summarize an event or a lesson in 140 characters or less. This can be a great way to get the students to streamline their summaries.

Mind Map

Figure 3.25 shows a sample mind map for the word *summarize*.

FIGURE 3.25
Mind Map for *Summarize*

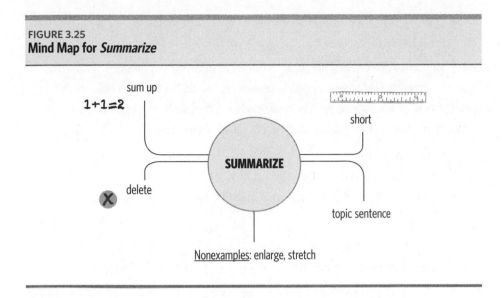

Paraphrase

Definition: put the author's words into your own words; make it easier to understand

♪ **Jingle:**   Paraphrase what authors say.
                 Make it easy   say it your way.

When asking students to compare *paraphrase* and *summarize*, try a simple trick. *Paraphrase* can be thought of as a pair of phrases, meaning more than one. *Summarize* is the sum total, like the sum of an addition problem. So *summarizing* is creating something short that covers the main points, while *paraphrasing* is changing the words of the author into your own words, a longer process.

Summarize = short ⟶
Paraphrase = long ⟶

- When I go back to school after the summer I must summarize what I did during the break.
- At a lecture I take notes and paraphrase what the speaker said.

Give students two index cards. Print *paraphrase* on one; *summarize* on the other. As you read work that is paraphrased or summarized, have students hold up the card they believe is representative of what you are reading. Initially you might use cues such as "To sum things up," or "Although these are not the author's exact words, I think the ideas are. . . ."

Other examples would be:

- Here is the main idea that the author was trying to share.
- I am not quoting here, but this is what the author said.

Graphic Organizer: Comparing *Summarize* and *Paraphrase*

Using a Venn diagram like that in Figure 3.26 or another graphic organizer to show the similarities and differences between *summarize* and *paraphrase* is a good idea. Teach each concept separately and then show the comparison.

FIGURE 3.26
Venn Diagram Comparing *Summarize* and *Paraphrase*

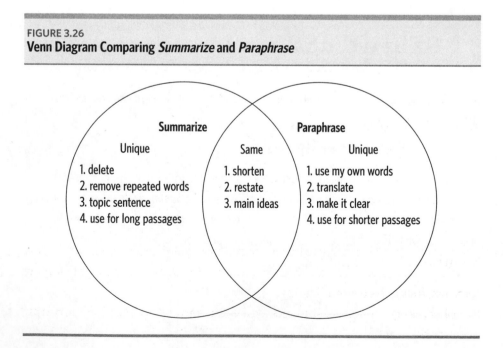

Summarize Unique	**Same**	**Paraphrase** Unique
1. delete	1. shorten	1. use my own words
2. remove repeated words	2. restate	2. translate
3. topic sentence	3. main ideas	3. make it clear
4. use for long passages		4. use for shorter passages

Support

Definition: hold up, prove, help

Synonym: back up, backing

Antonym: oppose, abandon

♪ **Jingle:**   Support! Support! Strengthen what you say.
             Hold up your thoughts in another way.

Movement: Have students move into groups of three. Two students hold the other student up as though he or she cannot walk well.

Support in the Common Core

The first College and Career Readiness Anchor Standard for Reading under Key Ideas and Details states:

1. Read closely to determine what the text says explicitly and to make logical inferences from it; cite specific textual evidence when writing or speaking to *support* conclusions drawn from the text.

The grade-level-specific standard for 2nd grade under Reading for Information reads:

RI. 2.8. Describe how reasons *support* specific points the author makes in a text.

Support in Webb

Webb's Depth of Knowledge levels shows the verb support at Level 3, Strategic Thinking. Whether used as a noun (show support) or a verb (support ideas), students must be able to think strategically to locate the right support for what they are communicating.

Most assessments ask students a question and follow with "support your answer with. . . ."

Introducing *Support*

I introduce this word by asking my students what they would do if they were hiking with two friends and one twisted his ankle. With no cellular service and the weather becoming inclement, how would they help their friend down the hill? After they mention words like "carry him," I ask for a demonstration. Many students want to participate and invariably almost all students rise, grab two of their classmates, and act out the scenario. It's a great way to discuss *support*. I ask one of the supporters to let go. We then discuss how helpful it is to have more than one support. Hence, the dialogue about support when we provide information ensues. From then on, the movement or kinesthetic way to define support is engrained in their brains.

Frayer Model

Figure 3.27 is an example of how support could be displayed in a graphic organizer such as the Frayer model.

FIGURE 3.27
The Frayer Model for *Support*

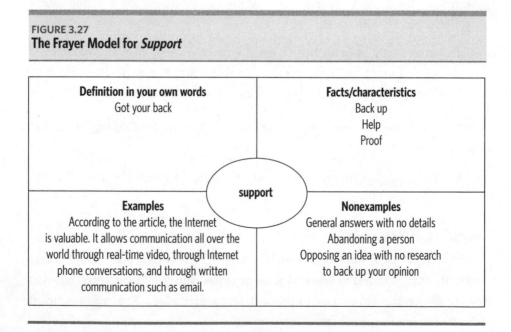

Definition in your own words	Facts/characteristics
Got your back	Back up Help Proof

support

Examples	Nonexamples
According to the article, the Internet is valuable. It allows communication all over the world through real-time video, through Internet phone conversations, and through written communication such as email.	General answers with no details Abandoning a person Opposing an idea with no research to back up your opinion

Drawing

Draw a picture that shows the vocabulary word and a rhyming word that makes the definition easier to remember.

> Example: The *support* for the *port* was weak.

The students would draw a port (harbor) that shows boats tied to docks with broken or weak ties.

Transforming *Support*

Have students add prefixes and suffixes to any of the critical verbs to see how the word may change. *Support* can become *supported* or *supporting*. Discuss whether or how the changes affect the definition.

Prove It!

Write some statements on the board that may or may not be true. Ask students to decide if they believe the statements. Whether they do or not, ask them to "Prove it!" This is an excellent way to bring in technology. Have students search the Internet for support of their claims. Here are sample statements:

- China is the largest country in the world.
- Nevada is called the "gold" state.
- A McDonald's hamburger has 300 calories.

The statements you choose should be appropriate to your grade level. Students may work in groups or alone. Your statements may be related to material you have covered or are currently teaching. Therefore, if Internet access is unavailable, your text or supporting materials may have the answers. Be sure to make notice of the "supporting" materials!

Synthesize

Definition: combine to form a more complex product

Synonyms: create, produce, combine, blend, make

Antonym: take apart

♫ **Jingle:**   To synthesize is to become the creator
            Of a product that is even greater!

Example:

- He synthesized old and new ideas.

Synthesize in **Webb and Bloom**

Synthesize is a Level 4 word on Webb's Depth of Knowledge as the expectation for Level 4 activities is to be able to analyze and synthesize information from multiple sources. On the old Bloom's taxonomy, synthesize is the second highest level of thinking; and on the new Bloom's taxonomy, it is the highest level of thinking labeled Creating.

Synthesize in the **Common Core**

Under Key Design Considerations in the CCSS, it states:

> To be ready for college, workforce training, and life in a technological society, students need the ability to gather, comprehend, evaluate, *synthesize,* and report on information and ideas, to conduct original research in order to answer questions or solve problems, and to analyze and create a high volume and extensive range of print and nonprint texts in media forms old and new.

Vocabulary Word Map Flipbook

A teacher shared this idea in one of my workshops. She had learned of the wonderful fact flipper idea of Tammy Worcester, author of *50 Quick and*

Easy Ideas for Kids, and she adapted it for vocabulary. I love it because it utilizes technology. PowerPoint is used to make this book, and other websites can be used to get clip art pictures or drawings. You can follow any of the vocabulary word maps and make a slide for each section.

- Open a blank PowerPoint presentation and choose the layout you want. I usually choose "Title Only" for this.
- On the first slide, type *Synthesize* in any color or font you like.
- Click "Add a Slide" and choose the same layout.
- Continue adding slides until you have six total.
- Slide 2, type in *Definition.*
- Slide 3, type in *Synonym.*
- Slide 4, type in *Synonym.*
- Slide 5, type in *Antonym.*
- Slide 6, type in *Sentence.*
- Add slide 7 and type in name and class (e.g., "Billy Jones, 3rd period").
- For Slide 8 type the definition of *synthesize* (e.g., "combine to form something new").
- Slide 9, type a synonym like *mix.*
- Slide 10, type a synonym like *create.*
- Slide 11, type an antonym like *divide.*
- Slide 12, type a sentence using the word *synthesize* ("I will synthesize the information from the poem and the passage to create another poem").
- The students can click "Insert, Clipart" and choose pictures to put on the pages, or they may look up pictures on the Internet or find some in magazines (pictures should be small).
- Save the Vocabulary Word Map Flipbook.
- Print the book as handouts.
- Page 2 contains the answers, so you will want to glue page 1 to page 2, *but* before you do that, take scissors and cut the page one slides on the sides and the bottom. That way, when the pages are glued together, you can flip up the "question" and see the answer.

See Figure 3.28, which shows the handout pages.

FIGURE 3.28
Handout Pages of the Vocabulary Flipbook

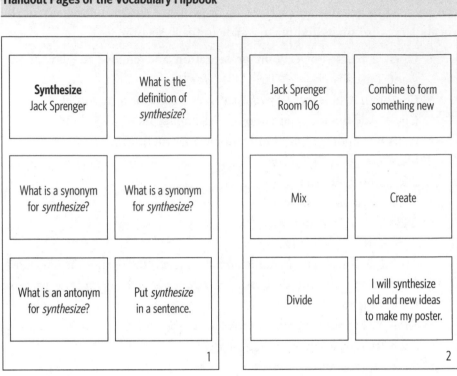

Trace

Definition: follow the course or development of; find or discover by investigation

Synonyms: outline, copy, sketch, find, track, follow

♫ **Jingle:**   Trace the steps from the start.
             Follow it, outline it, part by part!

Trace in the Standards

Standard 8 of the Reading Standards for Informational Texts 6–12 is:

> RI.6.8. *Trace* and evaluate the argument and specific claims in a text, distinguishing claims that are supported by reasons and evidence from claims that are not.

Appendix B of the CCSS:

> Students *trace* the line of argument in Winston Churchill's "Blood, Toil, Tears and Sweat" address to Parliament and evaluate his specific claims and opinions in the text, distinguishing which claims are supported by facts, reasons, and evidence, and which are not. [RI.6.8]

Modeling

Modeling is a popular way to begin teaching students a process. Bring in an argument or explanation from a newspaper, magazine, or online resource. Read the text to the class and think aloud as you do so. Explain to students what the argument or explanation is about. As you find evidence to support the argument or information that shows the steps in the explanation, let students know what is going on in your mind.

Hand out to the class the same text you just read and shared. Have students trace the argument or explanation, underlining key words or ideas.

Then put students in small groups of three or four and have them share what they found. Give them several minutes to evaluate the evidence.

Learning to Trace Arguments and Explanations

One way to start this process is by studying the transition words or "signal" words used in an argument.

Chronological (words about the order of things)

- First, second, third
- Next, then
- After
- Following

Cause-Effect (words about things that make other things happen)

- So, thus
- Therefore, hence
- Consequently
- Due to
- Example (words to show what a thing is)
- One such, another
- For instance, for example

Addition (words that add more information)

- Similarly, additionally
- Another
- Also
- Moreover

Opposition (words that signal a conflict or problem)

- But, though, however
- On the other hand
- Conversely
- Yet
- Nonetheless, nevertheless

Have students write a short argument. Tell them that they must have valid support for their statements and that they should use the transition words that go along with the type of argument they are presenting.

Editorialize

Give your students the following assignment:

1. Find an editorial from your local newspaper (either in print or online).
2. Read the essay.
3. Underline the transition words (for an online article, write down the transition word). Think about which category each transition word would fit into (chronological, cause-effect, etc.).

4. Now, take the transition words *out* of the essay.
5. Read the essay again. What effect does that have?

Concept Map

A graphic organizer will be helpful for learning this word (see Figure 3.29).

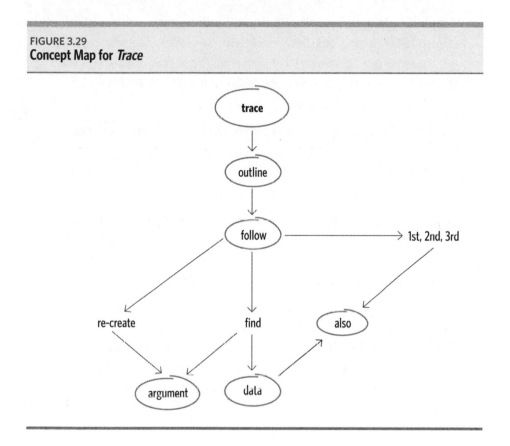

FIGURE 3.29
Concept Map for *Trace*

Review Game #4: Word Wall Spies

Do you remember playing "I Spy with My Little Eye" as a child or with your child? This game is a take-off on that entertaining game. If your critical word wall has the words in just one color, you simply go with the definition like this.

"I spy with my little eye a word that means. . . ." You then put in your definition, and students raise their hands and you call on one. However, to make things fair and to use this as a review quiz, I often draw the student's name from a bowl or have popsicle sticks with their names on them in a container on my desk. Hopefully everyone has learned the words and this is an easy, stress-free review.

If you have made a word wall with the words in various colors, you can narrow the field by saying, "I spy with my little eye a purple word that means. . . ." This may be helpful in the beginning of the critical word study. Later, you may want to keep your colorful wall, but not give the color clues.

To extend the review, you may want the student who provides the first word to continue the game by choosing the next word and giving its definition. This provides more reinforcement for the long-term memories. If you have the time, a second student may be called upon to give an example, a synonym, or an antonym.

This review game is a great formative assessment. I often have students write down the words they don't know, even for the words that they were not personally asked about. I try to make sure that I make time for the vocabulary learning centers for those students who need more practice.

CHAPTER 4

The Critical Words:
The Nouns

You have accomplished a lot if your students now know the critical verbs that will raise their test scores, improve their vocabularies, and enhance their communication. As far as the CCSS are concerned, you have helped students reach major milestones toward their success.

Why the nouns? As you look at the list in Figure 4.1, you will recognize words that you use throughout your teaching if you are an English/language arts teacher. (Many of these words are also used in other content areas.) You may have taught your students how to present an argument, but do they know what an argument is? Most students will reply, "It's a fight." There is nothing wrong with that definition, except that it's the wrong definition for your purposes. If we look at how and how many times these words are used in the CCSS, we can instantly see the importance of getting these words into long-term nonmotor procedural memory.

You will want to pre-assess your students with the nouns, as you did in Chapter 3 for the critical verbs (see Figure 4.1). This pre-assessment will give you an idea of how many words will need to be addressed. Although some of the words are not included in the CCSS until 3rd, 4th, or 5th grade, many of them are, or should be, introduced as early as kindergarten.

FIGURE 4.1
Pre-Assessment for the Critical Nouns

Word	I don't know it	I might know it	I know it!
Alliteration			
Analogy			
Argument			
Central Idea			
Conclusions			
Connections			
Connotative Language			
Details			
Evidence			
Figurative Language			
Illustrations			
Metaphor			
Mood			
Point of View			
Rhetoric			
Simile			
Stanza			
Structure			
Theme			
Tone			

The Nouns

The critical nouns are not equal. Some of them we can incorporate into teaching dialogue and on assessments, but others are specific to a certain content or skill and may require a bit more time and practice. For instance, even though we use *metaphor* and *simile* on a daily basis, we don't generally call attention to these words unless we are teaching specifically these figures of speech or we are considering the power of a speech or letter written by a famous person. We may use them again if students are writing narratives or essays. When my history students were writing essays, did I remind them to use metaphor? I don't think so. I reminded them to use key ideas and details and to show evidence for their writing, but I didn't go into figures of speech. Would that have made their writing stronger? Absolutely! The best writers in history class probably did use figurative language, and that made reading their essays more enjoyable. Figure 4.2 is a list of the nouns and their definitions. Keep in mind that you may want to change a definition based on the grade level you are teaching.

The Order of the Introduction of the Nouns

As in Chapter 3 and those 29 verbs, I am providing the order in which these 21 nouns appear in the CCSS:

1st: *connections, details*
2nd: *alliteration*
3rd: *central/main idea, illustration, point of view, stanza, theme*
4th: *conclusion, evidence, figurative language, metaphor, simile, structure*
6th: *argument, connotative language, mood, tone*
7th: *analogy*
8th: *rhetoric*

Keep It Fun!

Nothing is more boring than learning vocabulary words in a straightforward, mundane way. I have tried to offer fun activities along with a few more serious ones. Let's face it, your students may only be using words like *theme*

FIGURE 4.2

The Critical Nouns and Their Definitions

Noun	Definition
Alliteration	Words in a row with the same initial consonant sound
Analogy	A similarity between like features of two things
Argument	A reason or set of reasons that something is true
Central Idea	Most important point the author makes
Conclusions	Summing up of an argument or text
Connections	Relating what you read to something else you know
Connotative Language	The association that a word brings to mind
Details	Isolated facts that support ideas
Evidence	Knowledge on which to base a belief
Figurative Language	Figures of speech used to make meaning clearer
Illustrations	Visual material used to clarify or add to a text
Metaphor	An indirect comparison
Mood	The way the author makes the reader feel
Point of View	The vantage point from which a story is told
Rhetoric	The art of writing or speaking effectively
Simile	A direct comparison using like or as
Stanza	A poetry term for paragraph; a section of a poem
Structure	Organization of a text
Theme	A unified idea
Tone	The author's attitude or outlook

ones. Let's face it, your students may only be using words like *theme* in your classes, but other words like *evidence, conclusions* and *details* will be used all of their lives. Make learning each of the nouns more fun with games, drawings, and the jingles. My students in middle school would teach other students the jingles when they got to high school. Students I didn't know would actually stop by my classroom and ask for help with the English vocabulary!

Differentiated Instruction

Figure 4.3 is used as a formative assessment for differentiation purposes.

And the Password Is . . .

A game like Password can be a great way to change the mood of your classroom and make learning fun. Here are the steps:

1. Divide the class into two teams.
2. Put two chairs in the front of the room with the backs to the screen or board that you will be using to display the words.
3. Display the word on the board or on the screen behind the contestants.
4. Ask for synonyms from the team members. This must be done in an orderly fashion. Decide which team will go first by flipping a coin. Then rotate the opportunity to give a synonym.
5. When one of the contestants says the correct word, the team gets a point. Ask for two more contestants and the game continues.

This is a great way to review as you are making your way through the list of nouns. You may want to throw in some of the verbs, too. Repetition is good for long-term memory.

Teaching the Nouns

The words are presented to you in this chapter alphabetically. It will be more important that you present these nouns to your students in the order in which you will be presenting corresponding material. I also took the liberty

FIGURE 4.3
Formative Assessment to Differentiate Teaching of the Critical Nouns

Word	My definition	My sentence using this word
Alliteration		
Analogy		
Argument		
Central Idea		
Conclusions		
Connections		
Connotative Language		
Details		
Evidence		
Figurative Language		
Illustrations		
Metaphor		
Mood		
Point of View		
Rhetoric		
Simile		
Stanza		
Structure		
Theme		
Tone		

of combining some of the words. *Figurative* and *connotative language* are offered together. Students need to know the differences between these, and it made sense to teach them together. There are separate jingles and separate activities for them. *Metaphor* and *simile* are presented together as well. Most teachers I consulted with agreed that although they prefer to introduce them separately, eventually students need to differentiate between the two. Again, there are separate jingles and activities, along with combined activities. Finally, *tone* and *mood* are in the same section. They are often taught together, and many times they are included in the same standards. The section is set up to be taught separately and together.

You can see that the definitions of the nouns are longer and more complex than those of the verbs. Change the definitions to fit your grade level and to suit your needs. The nouns, however, require more explanation in most cases. For instance, *figurative language* has its own definition, but it includes many other vocabulary words for students to learn: *idioms, hyperbole,* and *personification,* to name a few. *Structures* are text structures, and there are many of them. It is important for every teacher to know about text structure and to teach his or her students what structure the text for the class uses. In history there are many problem/solution and cause/effect structures to explain our past. Therefore, check the words out carefully to see if they apply to your curriculum.

Alliteration

Definition: words in a row with the same initial consonant sound (The same sound starts words and syllables.)

♫ **Jingle:**   Alliteration allows a sound
To actually astound!

Alliteration in the Common Core

In the CCSS, students are expected to know and identify alliteration by grade 2.

In the Reading Standards for Literature K–5, the 2nd grade version of Anchor Standard 4 states:

> RL.2.4. Describe how words and phrases (e.g., regular beats, *alliteration*, rhymes, repeated lines) supply rhythm and meaning in a story, poem, or song.

Examples of Alliteration

The good news is that most students enjoy alliteration. Once they can pronounce it, creating alliterative sentences and finding them in a text becomes a game. Whatever grade level you teach, you will need some examples.

For the Young

Betty Botter by Mother Goose

- Betty Botter bought some butter, but, she said, the butter's bitter; if I put it in my batter it will make my batter bitter, but a bit of better butter will make my batter better.

Three Grey Geese by Mother Goose

- Three grey geese in a green field grazing; grey were the geese and green was the grazing.

Tongue Twisters

- Peter Piper picked a peck of pickled peppers. A peck of pickled peppers Peter Piper picked. If Peter Piper picked a peck of pickled peppers, how many pickled peppers did Peter Piper pick?
- How much wood would a woodchuck chuck if a woodchuck would chuck wood? A woodchuck would chuck all the wood he could chuck if a woodchuck would chuck wood.
- Silly Sally swiftly shooed seven silly sheep. The seven silly sheep Silly Sally shooed shilly-shallied south. These sheep shouldn't sleep in a shack; sheep should sleep in a shed.

Classic Literature

The Raven by Edgar Alan Poe

"Deep into that darkness peering, long I stood there wondering, fearing, Doubting, dreaming dreams no mortal ever dared to dream before."

Purple Penguins

This game comes from *Games for Reading* by Peggy Kaye (1984). I have played it with classes at all levels. We play the game first, and then I explain alliteration. "Purple penguins pick pineapples" is a true Purple Penguin sentence because all of the words begin with the same sound. Some teachers play Purple Penguins and do not allow any words that begin with a different consonant sound; however, for alliteration it is acceptable to do this.

Example: Harry's hamster ran into the hallway.

Alliteration Bubble Art

Have students draw a bubble map like the one in Figure 4.4. In the center bubble put a letter. Add four bubbles surrounding the center one. In each

FIGURE 4.4
Alliteration Bubble Art

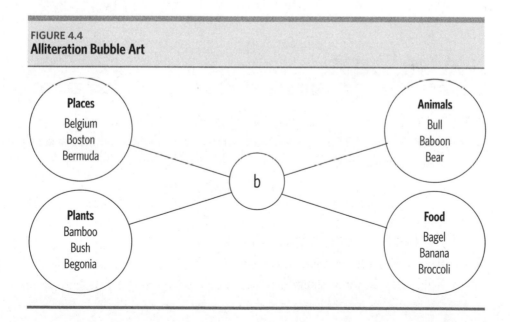

bubble write a topic such as animals, plants, food, and places. As a class, fill in the bubbles with three to five words that begin with the same sound as the letter in the center bubble.

Alliterative Add-ons

This is a fun activity that the students can do in small groups or as an entire class. You have probably played the game in which one student starts a sentence or story and the next student adds to it. In this version, the first student begins the story using one letter as the initial sound of most words. So, if Susan says, "Sally smelled something stinky on the stove," the next student might add, "Spaghetti sizzled in sister Susie's stainless steel saucepan."

Funny Friends

This is a familiar activity for alliteration. Have students write a sentence about their friends using alliteration.

> My friend Lori likes licking lollipops.
> My friend Sam sometimes skips to school.

Analogy

Definition: figuring out how things are related; a similarity between like features of two things, on which a comparison may be based; when two different things share characteristics that lead to a comparison between them

Synonyms: parallel ideas, correlation, comparison, similarity, likeness

Example:

- *This* is to *that* as *what* is to *which*

♪ **Jingle:**   A is to B as C is to D;
I can make an a-nal-o-gy!

Identifying similarities and differences has been said to be the number one way to raise student achievement (Marzano et al., 2001). Analogies fall into this category. Analogies help us look at things that appear dissimilar and find their similarities. Analogies develop logic. They also help students analyze words and find relationships between them. In our minds we may think A is to B as C is to D (A:B::C:D); school is to child as work is to adult; A is to B as 1 is to 2.

Types of Analogies

Relationships between words differ; therefore, knowing the relationship of the first pair of words assists us in understanding or creating the second pair.

- Synonym: one word means the same as another (lose is to misplace as walk is to stroll).
- Antonym: one word means the opposite of another (happy is to sad as tall is to short).
- Part and whole: the first word of each pair is part of the second word (wheel is to bicycle as chapter is to book).
- Whole and part: the second word of each pair is part of the first word (stove is to burner as airplane is to wing).
- Characteristic: a quality of one item is like the quality of the second (glass is to smooth as sandpaper is to rough).
- Classification: one word in each pair classifies the other word (car is to transportation as polka is to dance).
- Cause and effect: one word causes the other (happiness is to smile as sadness is to frown).
- Function: one word describes the function of the other (scissors is to cut as pen is to write).
- Location: one word tells you where you can find the other (ocean is to fish as kennel is to dog).

Animal, Vegetable, or Mineral

Teaching young students to create or complete analogies can be fun for all. Begin with animals because most students are fairly familiar with them.

- Fish is to swim as bird is to fly.
- Dog is to run as rabbit is to hop.
- Broccoli is to green as corn is to yellow.

Vocabulary Word Map

See Figure 4.5 for a sample of *analogy* in a word map.

FIGURE 4.5
Vocabulary Word Map for *Analogy*

Write the word.	analogy
Write a definition of the word.	a similarity between features of two things that can be compared
Write a synonym.	similarity, likeness
Write an antonym.	dissimilarity, unlikeness
Write the word here, in color.	
Use the word in a sentence that shows its meaning.	If you make or draw an analogy between two things, you show that they are alike in some way.
Draw a picture showing the meaning of the word.	

Analogy Match-up

On large index cards or on notebook paper, write the first part of an analogy, and write the second part on a second card or piece of paper. If you have several classes in which you would do this activity, I would do this on stronger cards, laminate them, punch two holes in the top and put yarn or thin rope through them. This way the students can wear them and they can be used forever. Have enough analogies so that each student wears one and has a person in the room that will complete the analogy.

Place a card face down on each student's desk. When all have been passed out, ask the students to stand, look at their card, hold it so that others can see it, and walk around looking for their match.

Option 1

After all think they have their match, have students stand with their partner and find a starting point. Each pair will read their analogy. Have them begin by saying "Our analogy is," in order to get the repetition of the word *analogy* into long-term memory. As they go around, if there is an incorrect analogy, you know there will be at least one more incorrect. You can have the class figure it out as a group.

Option 2

As the students are pairing up, when you see an incorrect pair, stop the game, and tell the class there are some errors and they should check their own and the analogies of others. In this way, no one is pointed out, and the students have the opportunity to self-correct and help others.

Examples

- crucial is to important   definitely is to absolutely
- rose is to flower   screwdriver is to tool
- liar is to honesty   fool is to wisdom
- teacher is to student   mother is to child
- refrigerator is to cold   stove is to hot

Critical Assembly

- Distribute one letter card to each student as students enter the class, or have them choose a card from a bag.
- When every student has a letter, call out a critical word that they have mastered.
- Students rush to find other students who have the letters they need to spell that word. The first group to line up in order is the winner, although you can set it up so that several words are still possible to spell out, and give the students time to assemble another word or two.
- Students must also write a sentence on the board demonstrating their knowledge of the meaning of the word.
- This process may be repeated with additional words as time permits.

Argument

Definition: a reason or set of reasons that something is true

Synonyms: case, reason, claim

🎵 **Jingle:**   Let's argue! Let's argue! But I don't want to fight.
I will find the facts to prove that I am right!

Argument in the Common Core

Appendix A of the CCSS states, "the Standards put particular emphasis on students' ability to write sound arguments on substantive topics and issues, as this ability is critical to college and career readiness." It also states, "in grades K–5, the term 'opinion' is used to refer to this developing form of *argument*."

Writing Standards K–5 note that in kindergarten, students are expected to:

W.K.1. Use a combination of drawing, dictating, and writing to compose opinion pieces in which they tell a reader the topic or the name of the book they are writing about and state an opinion or preference about the topic or book (e.g., *My favorite book is . . .*).

Anchor Standard 8 in the College and Career Readiness Anchor Standards for Reading:

8. Delineate and evaluate the *argument* and specific claims in a text, including the validity of the reasoning as well as the relevance and sufficiency of the evidence.

In the Anchor Standards for Writing K–5, you will find:

1. Write *arguments* to support claims in an analysis of substantive topics or texts, using valid reasoning and relevant and sufficient evidence.

An example from Appendix B:

Students trace the line of *argument* in Winston Churchill's "Blood, Toil, Tears and Sweat" address to Parliament and evaluate his specific claims and opinions in the text, distinguishing which claims are supported by facts, reasons, and evidence, and which are not. [RI.6.8]

Students may confuse argument with a fight, which is probably what they have heard throughout their lives. Students also confuse argument with debate or opinion. A proper academic argument involves critical thinking.

Argument in Webb

In Webb's Depth of Knowledge levels, developing an argument is a Level 3 skill that involves strategic thinking.

Not Persuasion

One of the five shifts the CCSS want us to make is this one: teach *argument,* not *persuasion. Persuasion* uses emotion to convince the reader; *argument* uses logic and reason. *Argument* has a thesis and evidence. Instead of asking students to write to persuade the school board to start school an hour later, ask them to write a research-based report that uses evidence to show that starting later in the day would be beneficial.

What Is the Purpose of Argument?

- To change the reader's point of view
- To bring about some action on the reader's part
- To ask the reader to accept the writer's explanation or evaluation of a concept, issue, or problem

Templates

The Gates Foundation is involved with the CCSS. One of the tools they have developed is templates. They have a template for a task requiring students to defend an argument based on evidence from informational texts (Phillips & Wong, 2012):

> Task 1. After researching _____ (informational texts) on _____ (content), write _____ (essay or substitute) that argues your position on _____ (content). Support your position with evidence from your research.
>
> - Level 2. Be sure to acknowledge competing views.
> - Level 3. Give examples from past or current events or issues to illustrate and clarify your position. (Argumentation/Analysis)

Teachers in all content areas can use this simple template.

Use Collaborize Classroom

This is a free collaborative education platform for students and teachers. Students can present arguments and theses in order to get feedback from the teacher and fellow students. Available at http://www.collaborizeclassroom.com/

Mystery Word

1. Select one of the critical words.
2. Write a "mystery" word on the whiteboard prior to class; cover each letter with an index card or sticky note.
3. Have students guess letters and reveal those letters by removing the cards one at a time like they do on *Wheel of Fortune.*
4. Students then will try to guess the mystery word with the fewest number of letters revealed.
5. After students have guessed the mystery word, ask for synonyms, antonyms, examples, definitions, and sentences.

Central Idea/Main Idea

Definition: most important point the author makes

Synonyms for main/central: chief, key, foremost

♫ **Jingle:**   What's the big idea you will find next?
The author's key point of his text!

Central Idea and *Main Idea* in the Common Core

The terms *central idea* and *main idea* are found throughout the CCSS and the exemplars in Appendix B.

Reading for Informational Text K–5

Grade 3:

RI.3.2. Determine the *main idea* of a text; recount the key details and explain how they support the main idea.

Determining the main idea begins in grade 3 for both the speaking and listening standards and the writing standards.

Appendix B

Students (with prompting and support from the teacher) read "Garden Helpers" in *National Geographic Young Explorers* and demonstrate their understanding of the *main idea* of the text—not all bugs are bad—by retelling key details. [RI.K.2]

Students provide an objective summary of Frederick Douglass's *Narrative*. They analyze how the *central idea* regarding the evils of slavery is conveyed through supporting ideas and developed over the course of the text. [RI.8.2]

Learning Begins with Long-term Memory

We are always asked to access prior knowledge when teaching a new concept. Prior knowledge is the information students have stored in their long-term memory. To get the main idea into their heads, begin with what they already know and like. What television shows do they all (or almost all) watch? Ask them about the main idea of a recent show. You can also assign a show to watch if all of your students have access to television. This may be a bit more difficult for your English language learners, so find out what they watch and see if you can make a connection.

So, What's the Big Idea?

Another way to reinforce this concept is to have children talk and write about what they know best: their family. Ask them what the "big idea" is about Grandma, Mom, Dad, a sibling, or another relative.

I got the following responses from kindergarteners:

- Jack: "The big idea about Gramma is she loves to be with me!"
- Emily: "The big idea about Mommy is she lets me bake with her!"
- Maeven: "The big idea about Daddy is he gets so excited when he sees me!"
- Darius: "The big idea about Uncle Julio is that he can fix anything!"

As students learn the big ideas about people are the main things they know or like about them, you can start to transfer the idea to what they read and write.

Give Them a Hand

A teacher shared with me an idea she uses that she found on the website Pinterest. She had the students trace their hand. In the palm of the hand they wrote the main idea of a story or poem. On the fingers they wrote the supporting details. The fingers need the hand to work, just as the details rely on the main idea, and the reverse is also true. This is similar to the vocabulary gloves, and it gives the students the opportunity for some movement and creativity.

At the Movies

After students have watched a movie, ask them to write one sentence to tell what the movie was about. Is this the main idea? Then ask them to write some details.

Conclusions

Definition: making up your mind based on evidence

Synonyms: determination, deductions, inferences, assumptions

🎵 **Jingle:**   If you jump to a conclusion,
You may cause some confusion.

Movement: Students jump forward and jump back.

Conclusions in the Common Core

College and Career Readiness Anchor Standards for Reading

1. Read closely to determine what the text says explicitly and to make logical inferences from it; cite specific textual evidence when writing or speaking to support *conclusions* drawn from the text.

Charades

Playing charades, or acting something out is a great way to teach young students about conclusions. Ask them to watch what you do and guess what it is. You can run in place, unscrew a jar, comb your hair, and so forth. Explain to them that when they are guessing, they are drawing conclusions from the evidence they see.

Step by Step

Read the first few sentences of a story aloud, stop, and ask students what they know so far. Tell them to listen to the names of the characters and their actions. Then ask them to draw conclusions about what they think the story will be about. Finish reading the story and ask students what they think the story means and what evidence they found to support their conclusions.

For Younger Students

Let students do interactive quizzes on drawing conclusions at Study Zone: http://www.studyzone.org/testprep/ela4/e/drawconclusionsp.cfm

Bring in Examples

Show students good examples of conclusions that previous classes have written. (Remove any names or ask for permission.) Show them some weaker conclusions as well. Have them discuss the following three issues:

1. How the conclusion gives emphasis to the "so what" and "now what" of the project
2. How the conclusion synthesizes rather than summarizes the information in the body of the paper
3. How conclusions "echo" but don't repeat the introduction

For Older Students

The website called Ending the Essay provides some good information for writing conclusions for papers. If students can write conclusions, they will be better able to draw them. See http://www.fas.harvard.edu/~wricntr/documents/Conclusions.html

Conclusion Chart

Create a graphic organizer conclusion chart like the one in Figure 4.6 as a class, or have your students create their own.

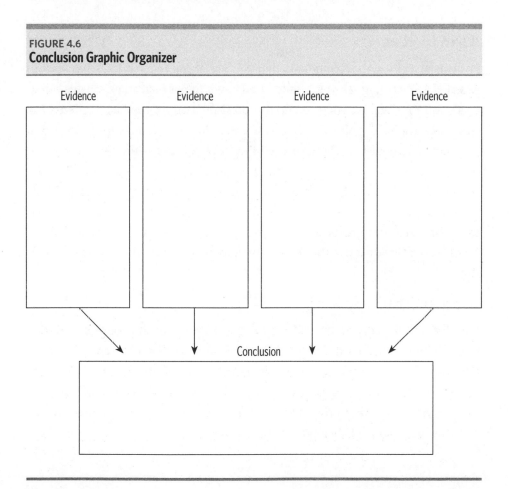

FIGURE 4.6
Conclusion Graphic Organizer

Conclusions from Movies

Kids love movies, and they like to let you know what they have gathered from them. Students probably draw conclusions often when they watch movies. Bring in a movie with an enjoyable scene from which students can draw conclusions (most movies will have a scene like this). Let students watch the scene and then work in groups to draw one or more conclusions from what they've watched. Encourage them to fill out a graphic organizer about one of their conclusions and emphasize the importance of basing their conclusion on facts from the movie.

It's in the Bag!

For this activity, you tell students that you are going to describe what various people have in a bag. The bag could be a brown paper bag, an expensive purse, or a shopping bag. As you pretend to pull things out of the bag, students can write down the details and then draw conclusions about the person. For example, you might say, "I have a red Prada bag here. Inside the bag is a tube of lip gloss, some eyeliner, a comb and brush, and a matching red wallet with five credit cards and $1,000 in it." You can continue describing bags and then have students work together to draw conclusions about several people, or do them one at a time (especially for younger students). When your students seem to get the idea, put them in small groups to design their own bags.

I Second That Emotion

For this activity, divide the class into groups. Give each group an emotion written on an index card. The group is to come up with a list of characteristics that would describe the emotion. For *sad* they may write "tear in their eyes," "a frown," and "sitting away from others." When they have their lists, they exchange with another group to see if the other group can draw a conclusion about what emotion is being described.

Connections

Definition: relating what you read to something else you know

Synonyms: links, associations, relations

♫ **Jingle**:   Make a connection; make a link,
              Use your head and think, think, think!

Connections in the Common Core

Language Standards K–5

Kindergarten: 5.c. Identify real-life *connections* between words and their use (e.g., note places at school that are colorful).

Appendix B

Sample Performance Tasks for Reading Informational Text

Students (with prompting and support from the teacher) describe the *connection* between drag and flying in Fran Hodgkins and True Kelley's *How People Learned to Fly* by performing the "arm spinning" experiment described in the text. [RI.K.3]

Sample Performance Tasks for Reading Stories and Poetry

Students make *connections* between the visual presentation of John Tenniel's illustrations in Lewis Carroll's *Alice's Adventures in Wonderland* and the text of the story to identify how the pictures of Alice reflect specific descriptions of her in the text. [RL.4.7]

Students make personal connections with the text by using their background knowledge. There are three main types of connections we make while reading text:

- **Text-to-Self (T-S)** refers to connections made between the text and the reader's personal experience.
- **Text-to-Text (T-T)** refers to connections made between a text being read to a text that was previously read.
- **Text-to-World (T-W)** refers to connections made between a text being read and something that occurs in the world.

Because most of the reading for college and career readiness involves complex informational text and the CCSS insist that students be able to read and make connections between multiple sources of information, it behooves us to focus on the text-to-text connections. Of course to begin the understanding of making connections at a young age, one source at a time makes sense.

To begin teaching about connections do a think-aloud. The think-aloud strategy allows you to model how a good reader thinks about text while reading. To model making connections, you can begin by reading something that is personally relevant to you. Students relate to nonfiction and informational text more than we appreciate, so use those to get them even more interested in these sources of information. As you read, stop and tell the students what you are thinking. With young students I begin by using the phrase "This reminds me of. . ." and share what I am thinking. Then I tell them that I just made a "connection" between the book and something else in my life or in another text. The next day, I read something that I think all of the children can relate to, and when I stop and say, "This reminds me of . . . ," I ask the students if it reminds them of something. Be sure to follow up with, "You just made a connection!" You want the word *connection* to get into long-term memory, and repetition will do it.

I follow the previous lessons with multiple books by a single author—an author study. We can then make connections between the author's books. The connections might be characters' personalities, story events, themes, settings, or messages.

Multiple authors on a similar topic is next. Bring in different genres: stories, poetry, drama, nonfiction, and informational text.

T-Chart

A simple T chart is helpful in getting students to focus on connections. On the left side of the T students write "Idea from the Text" and on the right side, "My Connection."

Getting Sticky

Sticky notes are often a staple when teaching students to make text connections. Students can mark ideas in their books with a sticky note that has the actual connection written on it, such as "This is like the theme in *The Giver*." The sticky may also just have the letters "TTS" (text to self), "TTT" (text to text), or "TTW" (text to world).

Find the Connection

Some teachers read through the text that their students will be reading in class and make sticky notes for text-to-text connections. When students arrive in class, they are grouped and each group receives one of the sticky ideas. They read through the text and try to find where the teacher found that connection. When they complete the task, the groups exchange sticky notes and look for the new connection.

Connection Brochure

A connection brochure can be made similarly to the booklet for the word *analyze* (p. 38). This paper-folding experience is fun, and students can use various texts to make their connections.

On the cover of the brochure students write "Connections" or "Connections Made Between_____ and_____," and put the titles of the texts on the cover as well. Have students draw a picture on the cover. Two drawings or pictures of books with arrows going back and forth between them is often easy to illustrate, although they certainly can draw whatever makes sense to them.

When the students open the cover, the back of the third section shows. Have them put the definition of *connection* in this area. Inside there are three columns. They can write TTS, TTT, and TTW at the top of each of these. Beneath those headings, they can write the connections they made from the texts they used.

On the back of the brochure, the students can write the title and a short summary of each text.

Connotative Language and Figurative Language

Definition of Connotative Language: the association that a word brings to mind; emotion determines the definition

 Jingle: Connotative meanings deal with emotion.
Word choice can be a powerful potion!

Definition of Figurative Language: changes the literal meaning, to make a meaning fresh or clearer, to express complexity, to capture a physical or sensory effect, or to extend meaning

 Jingle: Simile, metaphor, onomatopoeia, idiom.
Figurative language makes learning fun!

Connotative and *Figurative Language* in the Common Core

College and Career Readiness Anchor Standards for Reading K–5 and 6–12

4. Interpret words and phrases as they are used in a text, including determining technical, *connotative,* and *figurative* meanings, and analyze how specific word choices shape meaning or tone.

Appendix B

Students determine the *figurative and connotative* meanings of words such as wayfaring, laconic, and taciturnity as well as of phrases such as hold his peace in John Steinbeck's *Travels with Charley: In Search of America*. They analyze how Steinbeck's specific word choices and diction impact the meaning and tone of his writing and the characterization of the individuals and places he describes. [RI.7.4]

Language Standards 6–12

L.6.5. Demonstrate understanding of *figurative* language, word relationships, and nuances in word meanings.

    a. Interpret figures of speech (e.g.,personification) in context.

    c. Distinguish among the connotations (associations) of words with similar denotations (definitions) (e.g., *stingy, scrimping, economical, unwasteful, thrifty*).

Figurative language is also called *figures of speech*. The most common figures of speech are these:

- A simile: a comparison of two dissimilar things using "like" or "as"
- A metaphor: a comparison of two dissimilar things that does not use "like" or "as"

Language Standards K–5

L.4.5. Demonstrate understanding of *figurative language*, word relationships, and nuances in word meanings.

Figurative Language

- Personification: treating abstractions or inanimate objects as human, that is, giving them human attributes, powers, or feelings.

  Language Standard 6–12
  Grade 6. 5.a. Interpret figures of speech (e.g.,personification) in context.

Justice is blind.

Sunshine crept into the room.

The city never sleeps.

- Hyperbole: exaggeration, often extravagant; it may be used for serious or for comic effect.
- Idioms: a construction of words or a phrase that means something different than what the words are literally saying, e.g., get out of hand, make ends meet

L.4.5.b. Recognize and explain the meaning of common idioms, adages, and proverbs.

- Onomatopoeia: a word whose sounds seem to duplicate the sounds they describe—hiss, buzz, bang, murmur, meow, growl.
- Oxymoron: a statement with two parts which seem contradictory; examples: sad joy, a wise fool, the sound of silence, or Hamlet's saying, "I must be cruel, only to be kind"

Idiom Fun

Have students figure out the meaning of the following paragraph. They should underline the idioms, write them down, and come up with the literal meanings.

I know you are under the weather, but I still expect you to pull your weight. I took you under my wing and I am not ready to throw in the towel. The only way I can make ends meet is if you rise to the occasion. I will pay through the nose if things get out of hand. I may sound like a tempest in a teacup or one card short of a deck, but I am tired of trying to get you motivated. I feel like I am banging my head against a brick wall.

Connotative Language

Put a sentence on the board like "He is my friend." Informative, but not emotional. Add some connotative meanings.

He is my *best* friend.

He is my *only* friend.

He is my *texting* friend.

Ask the class for other suggestions. Then ask, "What does connotative language do to the meaning?"

Chicks and Dudes: What Do You Think?

Write on the board:

The woman walked down the street.

Then change the word *woman* to *chick*. Does the meaning of the sentence change?

The dictionary definition (also called the denotative meaning) is a person of the female gender.

What is the connotative meaning of each sentence?

Connotative Meanings: Worth Fighting For?

When people have fights over what someone said, it is often the connotative meaning that they are fighting over.

✜ Review Game #5: Mapping Memories

You may have encouraged your students to make mind maps of many of the words that they are learning. What about group maps of a handful of the words for review?

For this learning experience, divide the class into small groups of four to six students. Give each group a large piece of construction paper or flip chart paper. Ask each group to create a mind map of several of the words they have studied. You provide the words and keep the number of words low.

This need not take more than 15 or 20 minutes depending on the number of words. If the students find some of the words have similar meanings, they can draw arrows or dotted lines between the words. Don't give too many hints as this is a time for review, recall, and creativity.

When each group is finished, hang the maps on the wall and give the students a chance to look at and discuss them. It is unlikely that there will be blatant mistakes because the maps were made by groups of students, but there may be some questions asked of the groups about their maps.

This activity is a great way for students to understand how others visualize the words. The pictures or icons will be different and may give students a new vision of the word which may make it easier for them to understand and remember the term.

Details/Key Details

Definition: isolated facts; points of information

Synonyms: facts, specifics, fine points, items

🎵 **Jingle:**   A detail is a fact
That keeps you right on track!

Detail in the Common Core

The importance of recognizing and using detail cannot be overstated. The progression of this learning can be easily identified in the CCSS.

Reading Standards for Literature K–5

Understanding key details begins in kindergarten and continues throughout the grade levels.

RL.K.1. With prompting and support, ask and answer questions about key details in a text.

Learning in relation to details in Reading Standards for Informational Text progresses through the grade levels like this:

- Grade 1 RI.1.2 Identify the main topic and retell key *details* of a text.
- Grade 2 RI.2.1 Ask and answer such questions as *who, what, where, when, why,* and *how* to demonstrate understanding of key *details* in a text.
- Grade 3 RI.3.2 Determine the main idea of a text and explain how it is supported by key *details;* summarize the text.
- Grade 4 RI.4.2 Determine the main idea of a text and explain how it is supported by key *details;* summarize the text.
- Grade 5 RI.5.2 Determine two or more main ideas of a text and explain how they are supported by key *details;* summarize the text.
- Grade 6 RI.6.2 Determine a central idea of a text and how it is conveyed through particular *details;* provide a summary of the text distinct from personal opinions or judgments.

The list of standards in which students must find and use specific details goes on through Literature, Writing, and Reading for Informational Text. The word *details* may very well be the most used word in the CCSS.

Modeling

It is very important to model finding important or key details in text. Begin by reading short nonfiction books to your students. After each book, share with your students the details that are in the book. Look at the list of important facts you state. Model for students your thinking as you choose the four most important facts. Share that different people might make different choices, but talk to them about your thinking behind the choices you make. After having read several short books and sharing the details, ask students to offer their ideas on important details.

Will the Important Details Please Stand Out?

Finding the important details in a text can be difficult if it is filled with details that are unimportant. Sometimes it is necessary to list every detail from a story on the board and cross out the unimportant ones. Dividing the class into two teams can be a fun way to work on this skill. Both teams read the text or you read it aloud. One team is in charge of listing every possible detail and the other team determines which details are important.

3-D Graphic Organizer

1. Have students select a book or short text (nonfiction) that they would like to read and write about.
2. After they have had time to read their book, have students list the important details.
3. Have students put a check mark by the four most important details. Remind students that they are going to have to think hard about which things are most important because there may be lots of new information in their book.
4. Give students a large piece of construction paper. Holding the paper in landscape position (do this with them), have them fold the paper in half, and then open it back up. Then fold each side toward the center and crease the folds. They will now have an organizer with four panels inside.
5. Have students write a detail at the top of each panel.
6. Have students make an illustration beneath each key detail. Ask them to label their illustrations.
7. Fold the sides of the paper back in so that the two outer flaps, which are blank, are showing. These flaps become the cover of the book. Have students write the title of their book, make an illustration, and write their names.
8. Have students share their booklets, explaining why they chose each of the details.

An Ear for Details

Use music to teach main ideas and details. Students of all ages love music. Play some songs like the following and see if students can recognize the details in each.

- "Unwritten" by Natasha Bedingfield
- "The Boys of Fall" by Kenny Chesney
- "I'll Be There for You" by The Rembrandts (*Friends* Theme Song)
- "That's What Friends Are For" by Dionne Warwick
- "Breakaway" by Kelly Clarkson
- "American Soldier" by Toby Keith
- "Let Them Be Little" by Lonestar
- "You Belong with Me" by Taylor Swift

Use a graphic organizer and let students work together on a few songs. Then have them work alone.

Evidence

Definition: knowledge on which to base a belief; facts or information helpful in forming a conclusion or judgment; details that support an assumption

Synonyms: proof, indications, confirmation

♫ **Jingle:** E-vi-dence is simply proof.
Without it, you may goof!

Evidence in the Common Core

Reading Standards for Informational Text K–5

RI.4.8. Explain how an author uses reasons and *evidence* to support particular points in a text.

Writing Standards K–5

W.3.8. Recall information from experiences or gather information from print and digital sources; take brief notes on sources and sort *evidence* into provided categories

Prove It!

Teaching students to support their ideas with evidence can be fun. In this activity students are divided into groups and given a piece of poster paper. Have them make three columns on the paper, labeling the first "The Claim," the second "What I Think Is True," and the third "The Proof."

Provide several claims that people believe are true because "they" said so. Here are some examples:

- Humans only use 10% of their brains.
- Carrots improve vision.
- Fish is brain food.

Student groups choose one of the claims and write it in the first column on their poster paper. They then discuss whether they believe the claim is true. Next comes the detective work. Students use the Internet, library, textbooks, magazines, or other sources to either support or refute the claim. For instance, if carrots don't improve vision, why not?

When students finish the activity, post the papers and have each group discuss their claim and their evidence.

Cinderella Dressed in Yellow Went Upstairs to Kiss Her Fellow

Perhaps you remember this old rhyme that was used for skipping rope. It would continue with "How many times did she kiss him?" Then the rope jumper jumped as many times as possible until she or he tripped up.

When I have used this activity, just the name brings up questions. "Is any of this true?" Reading a short version of the Cinderella story, I provide questions afterward. They may be literal, as in "What were Cinderella's shoes made of?" "How did Cinderella get to the ball?" Then they become a bit more abstract to get the students thinking. "Was Cinderella happy at the beginning of the story?" "At the end?" After answering any of the questions, the students are asked to find evidence in the story to substantiate what they say. Some of the questions may require some inference, but of course, reading between the lines provides the evidence. (At the beginning, she was sad . . . she was crying.)

Think Like a Detective

In this activity teachers provide special boxes of evidence. In groups, the students open the box and look at the information inside. There will be pictures that might indicate the character's interests. Quotes may be included that help the students figure out what the character does. Symbols may be found that show what feelings the character has. Students look at the contents of the box and create a character.

For a real person the box may contain the following:

- A picture of a microscope
- A drawing of a brain
- A sheet of mathematical equations
- A pair of glasses
- A quote that says, "I did not like my brain traveling around the country."
- A miniature violin
- A comb
- A compass

These all are characteristics or have something to do with the life of Albert Einstein.

Providing a box with objects with no certain character in mind gives the students more freedom to be creative. They must provide a name for the character, an occupation, interests, and evidence of his or her feelings about something.

Illustrations

Definition: visual material used to clarify or add to a text

Synonyms: art, pictures, photos, diagrams, graphics, representations, examples, charts

♫ **Jingle:**   Illustrations add to the reading—
Important info you'll be needing!

Illustrations in the Common Core

The importance of illustrations cannot be overlooked. One may think that illustrations are simply pictures that are put in a story to make it more interesting, but they are much more than that. Illustrations include any art, graphics, charts, photos, or examples that are not placed within the text. Oftentimes these are critical for making sense of the text. Unless teachers in every content area model reading the text and supplemental materials and thus explain the importance of the illustrations, students may overlook them entirely.

In the real estate market, a home can have "curb appeal," making the property look more charming. In a text, that charm may also be used to keep the vocabulary level lower and easier to read. The difficult vocabulary (usually Tier 3 words) may be illustrated, so that the reader understands the idea without having to know yet another difficult vocabulary word that could slow down reading (Elster & Simons, 1985).

For the CCSS, your students will need to be able to glean information from illustrations. They will also need to determine if the illustration adds information to the text.

Teaching students about illustrations requires practice in reading graphs and charts, critically looking at drawings, illustrations, artwork, and any other visuals that may be provided.

In Appendix B of the CCSS Sample Performance Tasks for Informational Reading is the following 1st task:

> Students use the *illustrations* along with *textual details* in Wendy Pfeffer's *From Seed to Pumpkin* to *describe* the *key idea* of how a pumpkin grows. [RI.1.7]

Beginning in kindergarten students are expected to be able to tell the relationship between illustrations and the story in which they appear (Reading Standards for Literature, L.K.5).

Write It! Draw It!

Have students make illustrations to accompany their fiction and informational text writing. Working in pairs, students read each other's work and study the illustration and determine if it adds to the writing, replaces information that would otherwise need to be included in the writing, or adds nothing at all. Be sure to have students label their illustrations.

Talk About Illustrations

Many texts include illustrations. In general, lower-level books have more illustrations to motivate students to read and to add to their comprehension as they learn to read. Discuss the illustrations in short stories, pieces of informational text, and nonfiction writing. How do students feel about those illustrations? How many of them pay attention to them? In the areas that you teach, how are the illustrations important? Be sure to point out to students the level of importance of those illustrations.

Illustration Wheel

Illustration is a great word for the synonym wheel that you see in Figure 4.7. Students need to know that when they see the word *illustration,* it may refer to any of these words.

FIGURE 4.7
Illustration Synonym Wheel

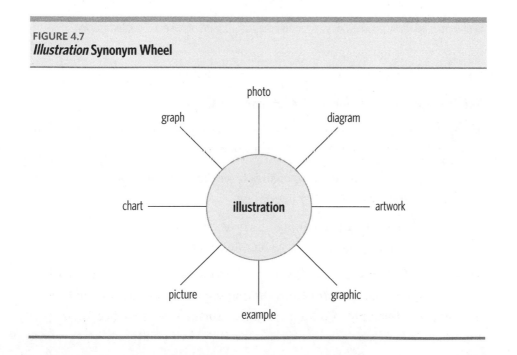

Transforming *Illustration*

This is one critical noun that has many forms that will be used on assessments and throughout students' lives. Talk about *illustrate, illustrating, illustrated, illustrative,* and *illustrator* with your students.

Metaphor and Simile

Definition of metaphor: an indirect comparison; an implied comparison using a form of the verb "to be," usually *is* or *are*

♫ **Jingle**:   A metaphor makes two things the same
                    By giving one the other's name!

Definition of simile: a direct comparison using *like* or *as*

♫ **Jingle**:   Use similes to compare;
                    Be sure *like* or *as* is always there.

Synonyms: no really good synonyms; sometimes use "figure of speech," comparison

Metaphor and Simile in the Common Core

Metaphor and *simile* are found in the Language Standards, Reading Standards, and Writing Standards—for example:

L.4.5a. Explain the meaning of simple *similes* and *metaphors* (e.g., *as pretty as a picture*) in context.

RI.5.5. Determine the meaning of words and phrases as they are used in a text, including figurative language such as *metaphors* and *similes*.

W.11–12.2.d. Use precise language, domain-specific vocabulary, and techniques such as *metaphor, simile,* and analogy to manage the complexity of the topic.

Understanding Metaphors and Similes

Metaphors and similes are figures of speech or figurative language. Figurative language changes the meanings of words by making them fresh and clear. Metaphors and similes have a similar job: to show how two things are alike. Similes tell you what something *is like*; metaphors tell you what something *is*. Similes use the words *like* or *as* to make a comparison. Metaphors never use *like* or *as*. To make them clear:

- Simile: "I was as cold as an ice cube." This is a comparison between me and an ice cube. It is much more descriptive than simply saying I was cold. I wasn't just cold; I was frozen!
- Metaphor: "I was an ice cube!" From the sentence you know that I was so cold I was frozen.

Authors use metaphors and similes to provide images of what they are writing. It makes the information come to life. Similes and metaphors are everywhere in literature and informational text. You know some by heart, but you probably didn't know that you know them. For example, "Mary had a little lamb; its fleece was white as snow." The wool on the lamb is being compared to snow because they are both white.

Many teachers introduce simile and metaphor together. I think getting one into long-term memory before introducing the other will help avoid confusion.

Simile Examples

You are as busy as a bee.
Run like the wind!
She is as stubborn as a mule.
He is as quiet as a mouse.

Making Comparisons: Similes

Write this on the board and give your students a copy.

Learning how to recognize and use similes is as easy as pie! Each and every one of you is as sharp as a tack. I will be as proud as a peacock when you are using similes in your writing. We will be as busy as bees while we are learning. Your ideas will ignite like fire!

Ask what they notice about the paragraph. Someone should come up with an idea about comparisons. Then discuss the definition of *simile* (a comparison between two things that are somewhat dissimilar using *like* or *as*). Have the students pick out all of the similes in the paragraph and discuss how the nouns are alike.

Alphabet Challenge for Similes

Put students in groups of three or four. Have one student in each group be the recorder. Have the recorders take a sheet of paper and write the alphabet down the left side of the paper with one letter per line. Then, tell the students that they are to use a word that begins with each letter to create a simile. Put examples on the board:

> A as angry as a bee
> B as big as an elephant

The first group to finish is the winner.

'Twas the Night of the Simile

As I was reading "The Night before Christmas" to my grandchildren, 4-year-old Emily asked, "Gramma, does Santa have roses on his cheeks?" Six-year-old Jack quickly responded, "Sure, Emmie, and he has a cherry on his nose!" and began laughing. He was responding to the line "his cheeks were like roses, his nose like a cherry." Take this poem and have your students find the similes. They can work in groups.

Introducing Metaphor

This is a fun way to talk about metaphor. Say the following to your students:

> We use metaphors every day! Have you ever described your brother
> in this way? "He is such a pig!" Can you picture his room a total
> mess? How about this statement: "He is so dreamy!" Do you think the

person who said this thinks he is attractive? Romantic? Perfect? This assignment will be a piece of cake. Think about what you say that would be considered a metaphor. Write the statements down and be prepared to share . . . or you might be toast!

Metaphors say a thing is another thing. Examples:

- My life is a nightmare. (The noun *life* and the noun *nightmare* are being compared.)
- I am a night owl. (Am I really an owl? No, but I am up late at night like an owl.)
- He is an early bird. (Is he really a bird? No. He gets up early like a bird.)
- Life is a journey. (How is this so?)

What Does It Mean?

We use metaphors on a daily basis and don't even think about it. Write sentences like the following on your chalkboard or whiteboard. Ask your students to think about what they mean.

David is a pig.
David is an angel.
David is a giant.
David is a shrimp.
David is a shark.
David is bright.

Making Metaphors

On your chalkboard or whiteboard write a list of words like the following, and ask your students to write a sentence with a metaphor to describe someone with that characteristic:

Tall
Fast
Smart

Angry

Stubborn

Scared easily

Silly

To Introduce Metaphor: "Life Is a Highway"

Play the song "Life Is a Highway," by Rascal Flatts. Ask students whether the title is a simile or metaphor. How could it be changed to a simile?

Similes and Metaphors in Music

Show your students the video clip "Similes and Metaphors in Music" available at http://www.watchknowlearn.org/Video.aspx?VideoID=50469&CategoryID=2258

This clip shows several pop music artists and their lyrics that contain metaphors and similes. It is an independent learning experience for students to do on their computers.

To Compare Metaphors and Similes

Write "Metaphor Master" on name tags for half of the class, and write "Simile Saver" on name tags for the other half. As students come in, randomly stick a name tag on the front of their shirts. Have the metaphor masters create a lesson on metaphors for the simile savers, and have the simile savers create a lesson on similes. By the time the students have researched their figure of speech, they will know it well. Have students present their lessons. For the rest of the day, whenever a metaphor is found, the metaphor masters stand up with their arms up like a champion and shout "Metaphor Master!" and the simile savers do the same.

Venn Diagram

Have students draw a Venn diagram comparing and contrasting *similes* and *metaphors* as we did for *paraphrase* and *summarize*. What the two have in common should go in the center.

Point of View

Definition: the vantage point from which a story is told

♫ **Jingle:**   Is it in first, second, or third?
                How did the author want to be heard?

Point of View in the Common Core

Appendix B of the CCSS Sample Performance Tasks for Stories and Poetry

When discussing E. B. White's book *Charlotte's Web*, students distinguish their own *point of view* regarding Wilbur the Pig from that of Fern Arable as well as from that of the narrator. [RL.3.6]

Students describe how the narrator's *point of view* in Walter Farley's *The Black Stallion* influences how events are described and how the reader perceives the character of Alexander Ramsay, Jr. [RL.5.6]

Students explain how Sandra Cisneros's choice of words develops the *point of view* of the young speaker in her story "Eleven." [RL.6.6]

Appendix B of the CCSS Sample Performance Tasks for Informational Text

Students determine the *point of view* of John Adams in his "Letter on Thomas Jefferson" and analyze how he distinguishes his position from an alternative approach articulated by Thomas Jefferson. [RI.7.6]

Students determine the purpose and *point of view* in Martin Luther King, Jr.'s, "I Have a Dream" speech and analyze how King uses rhetoric to advance his position. [RI.9–10.6]

College and Career Readiness Anchor Standards for Reading Literature

6. Assess how *point of view* or purpose shapes the content and style of a text.

The progression of point of view through grades 3, 4, and 5:

6RL.3.6 Distinguish their own *point of view* from that of the narrator or those of the characters.

RL.4.6. Compare and contrast the *point of view* from which different stories are narrated, including the difference between first- and third-person narrations.

RL.5.6 Describe how a narrator's or speaker's *point of view* influences how events are described.

Point of view is found in grades 6 through 12 and is also found in the standards for informational text, writing, and speaking and listening.

Huff and Puff

Activate long-term memory by asking your students if they have ever read "The Three Little Pigs." Call on a few students to share the story. The stories will probably be somewhat different. Discuss if the differences are a result of memory or point of view. Next, read "The Three Little Pigs" and discuss with your students who is telling the story. Then you can read "The True Story of the Three Little Pigs," which is told from the wolf's point of view. Let your students discuss the differences and similarities. You may wish to create a Venn diagram to compare the stories.

What Happened?

Have a member of your staff run into your room while you are teaching and take a stapler or some other item off your desk and then run out. Ask your students what happened. Have them write down their point of view of the incident and share what they wrote. Make sure they begin their account with "From my point of view." Discuss point of view.

Person to Person

A story can be told from a first-person, second-person, or third-person point of view. Review each of these points of view. Find a newspaper article that involves different people but basically contains the facts: who, what, where, and how. Assign each student a point of view—first, second, or third—and have them rewrite the article in a story format from that viewpoint.

Rhetoric

Definition: language designed to have a persuasive or impressive effect on its audience; the art of writing or speaking effectively

♫ **Jingle:**   You will do what I say
                   If I write in a rhetorical way!

Rhetoric in the Common Core

College and Career Anchor Standards for Speaking and Listening

3. Evaluate a speaker's point of view, reasoning, and use of evidence and *rhetoric.*

Sample Performance Tasks for Informational Texts: English Language Arts

Students determine the purpose and point of view in Martin Luther King, Jr.'s, "I Have a Dream" speech and analyze how King uses *rhetoric* to advance his position. [RI.9–10.6]

Students analyze Thomas Jefferson's Declaration of Independence, identifying its purpose and evaluating *rhetorical* features such as the listing of grievances. Students compare and contrast the themes and argument found there to those of other U.S. documents of historical and literary significance, such as the Olive Branch Petition. [RI.11–12.9]

What Is Rhetoric?

There are literally hundreds of rhetorical devices. Some of them are the figures of speech or figurative language that are mentioned in this book. Some consider rhetoric simply the art of persuasion.

There are different ways a writer can appeal to and seek to persuade his or her audience: (1) logic or reason (*logos*), (2) emotion (*pathos*), and/or (3) ethics and morals (*ethos*).

- **Logos:** appeals to an audience's sense of reason and logic; the writer intends to make the audience think clearly about the sensible or obvious answer to a problem
  For logos the writer relies on facts, statistics, definitions, historical proof, and quotes from "experts."
- **Pathos:** appeals to the audience's emotions; the writer can make the audience feel sorrow, shame, sympathy, embarrassment, anger, excitement, or fear.
  Pathos appeals to the audience through the use of figurative language, imagery, vivid descriptions, an emotional choice of words, or examples that encourage them to feel something.
- **Ethos:** appeals to the writer himself or herself; it is important that this person have impressive credentials, a notable knowledge of the subject, or appears to be a likeable and moral person.
  Ethos appeals to the audience with a calm, trustworthy, sincere approach. The writer uses good grammar, is well-spoken, and tells stories that are backed by general common sense.

Commercials

When talking about the art of persuasion, have students think of commercials that they see on television or on the Internet. Do they use pathos, logos, ethos, or a combination of techniques? Consider showing the students an infomercial for exercise equipment or makeup. How do the infomercials persuade the audience to buy products?

He Had a Dream

Dr. Martin Luther King Jr.'s "I Have a Dream" speech is used in the example from the CCSS. Because it is such an appealing speech, it is a good document for students to study and find rhetorical devices.

Teaching Rhetoric

- To teach the topic of rhetoric as it relates to composition, provide the class with reading examples so that they can see what rhetoric is and how to identify it in written bodies of work.
- Offer a few samples so that students get diverse exposure to different types of rhetoric, such as humorous, political, or philosophical rhetoric.
- After students read the examples, discuss the things that the compositions have in common as far as the rhetorical characteristics are concerned. Being able to identify rhetoric, or distinguish between effective rhetoric and ineffective rhetoric, is a suitable transition to teaching students how to write rhetoric.

Review Game #6: Cube It!

Create a cubing exercise to review six words at a time. You can use this review game when your students know at least six of the critical words. When they have learned multiples of six, you can create different cubes for every six words. Feel free to repeat some words that may be challenging on some of the cubes. For instance, if my students have difficulty distinguishing *describe* and *demonstrate*, I will put each of these words on multiple cubes for extra review. For cubing individual words, you may use these six components:

1. Definition of the word
2. Synonyms for the word
3. Antonyms of the word

4. Use the word in a sentence

5. Act out the word

6. Apply the word

When you are reviewing multiple words, your approach will be different. For example:

- Simply put six words on the cube, have students roll, and whichever words comes up, they give a definition.

- Put six words on the cube and call it a synonym cube. When it is rolled, the student must give a synonym for the word.

- Put definitions on the cube. Whichever definition comes up, the student provides the word.

- Put sentences on the cube that have blanks to fill in with one of the critical words. This can create good discussion as multiple words may fit the sentence.

- Create multiple cubes. Students who have difficulty with certain words will use a cube with those words. Be sure to put a few words on the cube that they are confident they know, so not all words are a challenge. Your students who are catching on easily to each word should be given cubes with the more challenging or most recent words to review. Students who already know all the words should have the most challenging cubes of all. Their cubes should be filled with higher-level activities or questions such as "Distinguish between the meanings of *distinguish* and *compare*" or "What type of graphic organizer could you use for *compare* and *contrast* besides a Venn diagram?" Cubes are a great way to differentiate instruction. When making multiple cubes, you may want to use different-colored paper for each. That way as you watch your students working, you will instantly know what level they are working on. If some students feel that they are being treated unfairly, assure them that they will be using the other cubes as soon as they feel ready to do so.

Stanza

Definition: a fancy poetry word for paragraph

Synonyms: verse, section

♫ **Jingle:**   A stanza is a room
           Where poetry can bloom!

Beginning in grade 3, students need to know what a stanza is and how stanzas relate to each other. *Stanza* is an Italian word for "room." One teacher shared with me that she explains to her 2nd graders that some poems have many rooms, like a big house, and some poems have only one or two rooms. The space in between the stanzas is like a hallway in a house or apartment. What a great simile! This is a comparison that all students could relate to in one way or another.

Stanza in the Common Core

Appendix B of the CCSS, Sample Performance Tasks for Stories, Drama, and Poetry

Students analyze how the opening *stanza* of Robert Frost's "The Road Not Taken" structures the rhythm and meter for the poem and how the themes introduced by the speaker develop over the course of the text. [RL.6.5]

College and Career Readiness Anchor Standards for Reading

5. Analyze the structure of texts, including how specific sentences, paragraphs, and larger portions of the text (e.g., a section, chapter, scene, or *stanza*) relate to each other and the whole.

Stanza Station

Take a poem appropriate for your grade level and write each stanza on a separate piece of poster board, large enough for students to see from their desks. Place the stanzas on the board out of order. Ask students to read the stanzas to themselves, or you can read them aloud. Ask students to consider whether the poem's stanzas are in the right order. Put the students in small groups and have them discuss the poem. How would they rearrange the stanzas?

Discuss how poems have beginnings, middles, and ends just like a story. Continue the discussion by asking what would happen if paragraphs in a story were rearranged.

Frayer Model

This graphic organizer is well suited for the critical noun *stanza*. See Figure 4.8.

George Co-stanza

If your students are fans of *Seinfeld,* they know George. George Costanza is Jerry Seinfeld's best friend and is quite a character. You could show a short

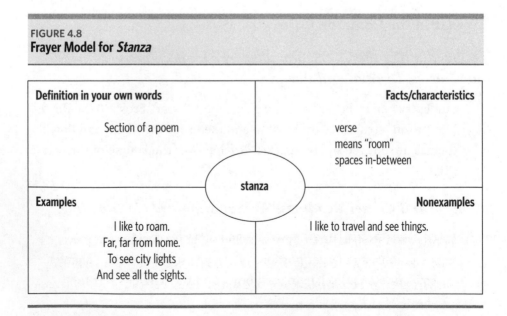

FIGURE 4.8
Frayer Model for *Stanza*

Definition in your own words	Facts/characteristics
Section of a poem	verse means "room" spaces in-between
Examples	**Nonexamples**
I like to roam. Far, far from home. To see city lights And see all the sights.	I like to travel and see things.

stanza

clip from YouTube and have your students write stanzas about George. This can be done in game form in which you brainstorm a topic for the "show," and have groups of students each write a stanza, or a co-stanza about George.

Structure

Definition: how the information within a written text is organized

Synonyms: arrangement, organization

♪ **Jingle:**   The structure of a text
                  Helps you know what will come next!

Movement: As students recite the jingle, they take their pointer fingers and form a shape, like a square.

Structure in the Common Core

College and Career Anchor Standards for Reading

5. Analyze the *structure* of texts, including how specific sentences, paragraphs, and larger portions of the text (e.g., a section, chapter, scene, or stanza) relate to each other and the whole.

Reading Standards for Literature K–5

RL.2.5. Describe the overall *structure* of a story, including describing how the beginning introduces the story and the ending concludes the action.

Reading Standards for Informational Text K–5

RI.4.5 Describe the overall *structure* (e.g., chronology, comparison, cause/effect, problem/solution) of events, ideas, concepts, or information in a text or part of a text.

The Importance of Structure

Teaching students these critical words in such a way as to get them into long-term procedural nonmotor memory, or automatic memory, is the basis for this book. Understanding text structure also assists with memory, and it does so by freeing up working memory. Learning about text structures and their signal words helps students understand and better remember what they read. As students go into higher grades, some of those signal words will disappear, yet the long-term memories they have about structure will allow them to understand the higher-level texts (Fisher, Frey, & Lapp, 2009).

Types of Text Structures

Although there are many text structures, for our purposes here, I will share the most common.

Cause and effect: explains how or why something happened

> *late for work, work not done, got fired*

Words that signal cause and effect: as a result of, in order to, for this reason, may be due to, so that, therefore

Compare/contrast: describes similarities and differences between two or more ideas, places, people, etc.

> *apples and oranges:*
> *alike: both fruits, both somewhat round*
> *different: flavors, colors*

Words that signal compare/contrast: in comparison, as well as, instead of, like, on the other hand, by contrast, by comparison

Chronological: in order of time, sequence, or describes a process

> *Stories are told in order of time: boy meets girl, boy marries girl, they live happily ever after*

Sequence: step 1, step 2, etc.

Words that signal chronological: first, next, meanwhile, later, second, third, later, after, before, soon, today, tomorrow, yesterday

Problem/solution: identifies an issue and resolves it

Can't find shoes, buy a shoe rack, don't lose shoes

Words that signal problem/solution: if, then, because, problem is, question is, solution is, answer is

Descriptive: outlines or lists details

Words that signal descriptive: such as, finally, above, beside, beyond, in addition, for instance, in back of, behind

Using Text Structures

- Introduce one of the structural patterns. Discuss the signal words and phrases that identify each text structure, and give students a graphic organizer for each pattern.
- Be sure to give students opportunities to work with the text. Provide the students with chances to analyze the text structures in informational books, not stories. This will help them learn the signal words and phrases in the text that identify each text pattern. They also may use graphic organizers to illustrate these patterns.
- Do a whole-class writing activity on one of the structures, followed by small-group, partner, and independent writing activities. Have students choose a topic and use a graphic organizer to plan the paragraphs. Then have the students write a rough draft using signal words (which they underline) for the text structure. Have students exchange papers with a partner to discuss the topic, the structure chosen, the signal words, and the overall clarity of the paper. Students then revise and edit the paragraph to produce the final product. Repeat these steps for each of the text structures.

Treasure Hunt

Have a text structure treasure hunt. Look for various text structures in newspapers, magazines, and textbooks. This can be done in small groups or individually once students are confident in their ability to find and use text structures. If using newspapers or magazines, have students highlight or underline the signal words.

Remember: we need our students to be able to use these text structures to aid in reading comprehension.

Theme

Definition: a unified idea carried through a text; the universal idea that an author is trying to get across

♫ **Jingle:**   Theme is the message you will find
                  Woven by the author through your mind.

Theme in the Standards

College and Career Readiness Anchor Standards for Reading

2. Determine central ideas or *themes* of a text and analyze their development; summarize the key supporting details and ideas.

9. Analyze how two or more texts address similar *themes* or topics in order to build knowledge or to compare the approaches the authors take.

Appendix B of the CCSS

There are numerous exemplars at all grade levels beginning with grade 5. Here are a few for Reading Literature and Informational Text:

Students summarize the plot of Antoine de Saint-Exupery's *The Little Prince* and then reflect on the challenges facing the characters in the story while employing those and other details in the text to discuss the value of inquisitiveness and exploration as a *theme* of the story. [RL.5.2]

Students analyze how the opening stanza of Robert Frost's "The Road Not Taken" structures the rhythm and meter for the poem and how the *themes* introduced by the speaker develop over the course of the text. [RL.6.5]

Students compare George Washington's Farewell Address to other foreign policy statements, such as the Monroe Doctrine, and analyze how both texts address similar *themes* and concepts regarding "entangling alliances." [RI.9–10.9]

Students analyze Thomas Jefferson's Declaration of Independence, identifying its purpose and evaluating rhetorical features such as the listing of grievances. Students compare and contrast the *themes* and argument found there to those of other U.S. documents of historical and literary significance, such as the Olive Branch Petition. [RI.11–12.9]

What Is a Theme and How Do You Find It?

What did the main character do in the story? This is the plot.

How did the main character's actions affect others in the story? This is the theme.

The theme of a fable is its moral. The theme of a parable is its teaching. The theme of a piece of fiction is its view about life and how people behave.

Theme is pulled out of a piece of fiction. The universal idea the author is trying to make is not stated explicitly. The action, setting, and characters lead the way to the theme. Theme can also be present in informational text.

Finding Theme

Students need a set of working themes. You want your students constantly considering *What is the author trying to teach me?* Consider supporting this with a theme wall. Post the universal themes listed here. Then, under each theme, list the corresponding texts you've read. You may also want to include titles of books students have read as part of the curriculum in previous grade levels. For younger students, you may want to reword this list or remove a few of the universal themes.

1. Man Against Nature
2. Man Against Man
3. Crime Does Not Pay
4. Overcoming Adversity
5. Friendship Is Dependent on Sacrifice
6. The Importance of Family
7. There Is Both Good and Bad in Life
8. Love Conquers All
9. Sacrifices Bring Reward
10. Human Beings All Have the Same Needs

I have found that sometimes it is easier to begin the idea of theme in informational text by providing the theme and having students, with my help and the help of the media consultant or librarian, find a book to fit the theme. It makes sense to provide more than one theme from which to choose. I base my choices on what fiction the students have read within those themes, either in my class or in previous classes. The students then have the opportunity to make connections between prior knowledge and new information.

Mnemonic for Theme

Theme is THE MEssage the author is trying to convey.

Tone and Mood

Definition of Tone: the author's attitude or outlook

Definition of Mood: the way the author makes the reader feel

♪ **Jingle:**   Tone is in the author's head.
          Mood is my feelings as I read!

Types of Tone: formal, informal, serious, humorous, amused, angry, playful, neutral, satirical, gloomy, conciliatory, sad, resigned, cheerful, ironic, clear, detailed, imploring, suspicious, witty

Tone and *Mood* in the Common Core

College and Career Anchor Standards for Reading

4. Interpret words and phrases as they are used in a text, including determining technical, connotative, and figurative meanings, and analyze how specific word choices shape meaning or *tone*.

Reading Literature Standards

RL.3.7. Explain how specific aspects of a text's illustrations contribute to what is conveyed by the words in a story (e.g., create *mood*, emphasize aspects of a character or setting).

Tone and Mood List

Authors can develop mood through word choice, dialogue, sensory details, description, and plot complications.

You can find an extensive list of tone and mood words at: http://s.spach man.tripod.com/SummerWork/tone_mood.doc

How Do You Feel?

If you have a poster with faces that show different feelings, teaching mood is a great time to use it. If not, create one using emoticons or pictures. Have students discuss the facial expressions associated with each feeling. What do these feelings have to do with mood?

At the Movies

Moviemakers try to set a tone for their movies. This should appeal to your students. Ask them how they think the tone is set for movies. Answers may include the dialogue, music, and lighting. Perhaps they will think of others. Show them the original *Mary Poppins* trailer found on YouTube at http://www.youtube.com/watch?v=fuWf9fP-A-U

After they watch, hand out a list of tone words and ask them to choose two words that might describe the tone of this trailer. Discuss their choices.

Go to the following web address to see the "Scary Mary Poppins" trailer: http://www.youtube.com/watch?v=2T5_0AGdFic. This is a shorter trailer that has a much different tone. Have students repeat the task with this trailer.

Head and Heart

To more easily get this point across, draw an outline of a person and write "tone" on the head and "mood" on the heart. You might simply draw a head and a heart on the whiteboard or chalkboard. This will remind students that tone is about what the author thinks and mood is how the author makes us feel.

Setting Examples

Show students examples of short writings or excerpts with various tones. Discuss the tones of each. Then:

1. Divide students into small groups.
2. Give each group a card with one of the following tone words written on it: *sadness, courage, tension, sympathy, love, happiness, pride, sarcastic, excitement, hate, fear, anxiety.*
3. Have each group write a description of a dog walking in the park, conveying the attitude on the card. They may not use the word written on the card in their description.
4. When writing is complete, instruct students to determine which tools were used to show tone in writing.
5. Ask each group to read the description.
6. Have other groups guess the tone.

A Trick to Distinguish Tone and Mood

Tone is the Author's ATTiTude
Mood is all about Me!

3-D Graphic Organizer

A trifold organizer like the brochure used with the word *analyze* works well for tone and mood. After the paper is folded, there are three columns on the inside. Write "Happy" at the top of the first, "Sad" at the top of the second, and "Angry" at the top of the third. On the front cover write "Tone," its definition, and add an illustration. Open the front cover and you are looking at the back of the third column; write "Mood," its definition, and an illustration. On the back of the brochure, have students write their names, class period, room number, or other information you need.

Using the list of tone and mood words, have students put the words in the appropriate columns. In groups have them share what words they chose for each category. As a homework assignment, students can find pictures to match each word.

Applying What They Have Learned

Assign stories and have students discuss the tone and the mood. In small groups, ask students to discuss how the tone and mood words affect the story. For students having difficulty, have them underline, highlight, or use sticky notes indicating where the words are located and whether they are tone or mood words.

Review Game #7: Magic Letter; Critical Word

This game is adapted from *Vocabulary Games for the Classroom* by Carleton and Marzano (2010). Providing students with a "magic" letter from the word you are asking them to think of makes the game more exciting, especially for the younger grades.

All you need is your chalkboard or whiteboard. Create a list of the critical words that you have studied thus far. For each word come up with a clue of some sort: synonym, antonym, definition, the jingle leaving out the word itself, or a sentence with the word. If you are using a movement for the word, you could use that as well.

Besides the clue, offer your students a "magic letter," which will be a letter in the word you are asking them to find. You might use the first letter, last letter, or any other letter in the word. The level of difficulty can be changed when you choose a letter. Many of the critical verbs begin with the letter "d," so you could make those easier by using the final letter. You may also want to designate whether the word you are looking for is a noun or a verb. You know your audience and can change the level of difficulty of the letter and the clues as you feel they have mastered the words.

Divide your students up into small groups

Write the letter and the clue on the board, along with the position of the letter in the word (beginning, end, or middle).

Tell the groups to raise their hands as soon as their team thinks they have the word. You can number the teams, give a point for each word, and keep score as you play.

Examples:

Clue: Break information down
Letter: first letter of the word is "a"
Answer: analyze

Clue: A is to B as C is to D
Letter: first letter of the word is "a"
Answer: analogy

Clue: Putting what the author says into your own words
Letter: last letter of the word is "e"
Answer: paraphrase

Clue: to judge
Letter: one of the letters in the word is "v"
Answer: evaluate

CHAPTER 5

The Last Words

You've looked through the CCSS and you see words that I have not included in the critical words, and you want to know why. I did make some choices as the word list got longer. For instance, words that begin in the lower grades and make their way through many standards and to the higher grades, I felt needed to be included. A few words that are certainly important—and perhaps critical—to your content and grade level also deserve a spot in this book. In addition, there are some adjectives and adverbs that our students need to know. So, this is the chapter for a potpourri of words.

Classify/Categorize

Definition of Classify: arrange in classes according to shared qualities

Synonyms: order, organize, sort

Definition of Categorize: putting classified items into smaller groups

Synonyms: catalog, label, group

Classify/Categorize in the Common Core

Writing Standard Grade 4. 8. Recall relevant information from experiences or gather relevant information from print and digital sources; take notes and *categorize* information, and provide a list of sources.

In the CCSS for Math, *classify* and *categorize* are found in kindergarten under Measurement and Data and continue throughout the grade levels in areas such as algebra and geometry, as well as in functions in high school.

Classify and Categorize in Bloom

Classify and *categorize* fall under the category of Analysis in Bloom's taxonomy: examining and breaking down information into its parts. Classify is also considered part of comprehension: demonstrating understanding of the stated meaning of facts and ideas.

The Category for Classify and Categorize

Identifying similarities and differences is a cognitive function that is fundamental to the brain. The brain likes to sort and organize learned information so it can connect it to incoming data. Our students learn by identifying patterns in their world and seek those same patterns to make sense of what is going on around them.

Explicitly teaching strategies for identifying similarities and differences is helpful for students. Not only do they need to have organizational patterns pointed out, they also need to be asked to construct their own strategies.

Students start out learning about patterns through sorting. They sort items by colors, size, use, and other key identifying characteristics. They begin to organize their brains with these broad groupings. Eventually the sorting activities are given names that differentiate them. Students begin to classify items and then categorize them.

Classifying and Comprehension

According to Silver, Dewing, and Perini (2012), inductive learning can begin with classifying. When students have difficult text to read, have them follow this process:

1. Make a list of the difficult and important words from the text.
2. Look up words whose definitions they do not know.
3. Work with partners or small groups of students to categorize each of the words.
4. Create word groups using all of the words.
5. Make predictions about what they think the text is about.
6. Discuss predictions with other small groups or as a whole class.
7. Read the text to see if predictions are accurate.
8. Show evidence supporting the predictions.

Classifying and Categorizing are both part of the research-based strategy Identifying Similarities and Differences (Marzano et al., 2001).

Explicitly

Definition: fully and clearly expressed

Synonyms: precisely, clearly

Antonyms: implicitly

♫ **Jingle:** Write explicitly—be very clear.
To the rules you will adhere!

Explicitly in the Common Core

The adverb *explicitly* is found throughout the CCSS.

Anchor Standard 1 for Reading

Read closely to determine what the text says *explicitly* and to make logical inferences from it; cite specific textual evidence when writing or speaking to support conclusions drawn from the text.

It is carried through the Reading Standards:

RL.3.1 Ask and answer questions to demonstrate understanding of a text, referring *explicitly* to the text as the basis for the answers.

RL.4.1. Refer to details and examples in a text when explaining what the text says *explicitly* and when drawing inferences from the text.

RL.5.1. Quote accurately from a text when explaining what the text says *explicitly* and when drawing inferences from the text.

One example from Appendix B:

Students explain the selfish behavior by Mary and make inferences regarding the impact of the cholera outbreak in Frances Hodgson Burnett's *The Secret Garden* by *explicitly* referring to details and examples from the text. [RL.4.1]

You can perform a search of the CCSS and see how often *explicitly* is used in the standards that pertain to you. You will find this word throughout.

I chuckled as I did a search on the Internet about how to teach the word *explicitly* because the hits that came up were all about teaching vocabulary explicitly.

Here is my lesson from my classroom:

Me: Today I want everyone to be explicit when they speak.

Student: Huh? What? What does that mean?

Me: I want you to give me clear information. When we discuss a chapter in history or science or literature, I want you to be explicit.

Student: I still don't get it!

Me: I want you to speak exactly.

Student: You mean, you want us to speak. Exactly, right?

Me: (sigh) Let me write this word on the board for you. Write it on your whiteboards. (They have small white erase boards.) Look at the word. When you speak or write, I want you to do so in a very clear manner. I want you to be precise in what you say.

Student: What is *precise*?

Me: It is a synonym for *explicitly*! (So, now I may be losing it, but I know they need to know this word.). Let's make a synonym wheel for *explicitly*.

Draw the wheel on your whiteboards as I draw it on the board up here. *Explicitly* goes in the center. Now let's come up with synonyms for each spoke of the wheel.

And so it went. We used *precisely, clearly, fully, exactly, accurately,* and *correctly.* Finally, they started to get it. We continued the lesson by making sentences. It worked!

Transforming *Explicitly*

Discuss other forms of the word with the students: *explicit, explicitness.*

Recognize

Definition: identify something you have seen before

Synonyms: know, spot

 Jingle: Recognize is something that I know;
I can spot it and make it show!

Students need to be able to do the following:

- Recognize when irrelevant information is introduced.
- Recognize and correct inappropriate shifts in pronoun number, gender, and person.

- Recognize variations from Standard English in their own and others' writing and speaking, and identify and use strategies to improve expression in conventional language.
- Recognize common types of text.
- Recognize idioms and other figures of speech.

Recount

Definition: give an account of an event or an experience; retell in detail and in order

Synonyms: retell, relate, report

 Jingle: Recount, relate, relay,
Explain it play by play!

Recount in the Common Core

At grade 2 the CCSS changes *retell* to *recount*. They begin expecting order and key details along with some support. Use the strategies for *recount* that you used for *retell*, and I will add a few that are more challenging.

Teaching *Recount*

Most teachers ask for some specifics when teaching *recount*.

- Write in the past tense.
- Have an interesting title.
- Have an introduction that includes Who? What? When? Where? How? Why?
- Tell details in order.
- Have supporting paragraphs.
- Write what people said, using quotation marks.

- Use connecting words to help the reader.
- Use powerful verbs and descriptive adjectives.
- Describe the feelings of the person telling the story.
- Have a concluding paragraph.

Share ideas and samples for each of these bullets with the class.

Order of Introduction of the Last Words

These five words first appear in the CCSS at these levels:

Kindergarten: *classify, recognize*
1st: *recount*
3rd: *explicitly*
4th: *categorize* (*category* in kindergarten)

Word of the Day

After having covered many of the critical words, occasionally assign each student one of the words for a day or several days. The object is to see how many times the student uses the word throughout the course of the day or days. When he or she uses the word correctly, the student gets a point or a sticker or whatever you think is appropriate. You can have them make individual sheets with their names at the top. They could have 10 or so spaces for words and columns to the side for checkmarks. As they have various words, they keep track of how many times they used each one and will be able to see which words are easier to put in conversation and which words they know best.

CHAPTER 6

Choose Your Words Wisely

In the Common Core Anchor Standards for Language under Vocabulary Acquisition and Use, there are three standards for us to consider:

4. Determine or clarify the meaning of unknown and multiple-meaning words and phrases by using context clues, analyzing meaningful word parts, and consulting general and specialized reference materials, as appropriate.
5. Demonstrate understanding of figurative language, word relationships, and nuances in word meanings.
6. Acquire and use accurately a range of general academic and domain-specific words and phrases sufficient for reading, writing, speaking, and listening at the college and career readiness level; demonstrate independence in gathering vocabulary knowledge when encountering an unknown term important to comprehension or expression.

What the CCSS refer to when asking that students acquire "general academic" and "domain-specific" words are the Tier 2 and Tier 3 words (respectively) that were presented in Chapter 1. Who is responsible for teaching these words? In the past, before the CCSS, teachers taught the Tier 3 words that presented themselves in the reading and lessons of their content area.

Because Tier 2 words are not domain-specific, no one quite knew who was supposed to teach them; and because most educators know and understand these words, they often assumed that the students also knew them.

In the Reading and Language Standards Related to Vocabulary K–5, there are more specifics as to what students should be able to do at each grade level. As you read these, note that the first letter or number is the grade level, the initials RL stand for Reading Language, and then the number that follows is the grade level.

RL.K.4. Ask and answer questions about unknown words in text.

RL.1.4. Identify words and phrases in stories or poems that suggest feelings or appeal to the senses.

RL.2.4. Describe how words and phrases (e.g., regular beats, alliteration, rhymes, repeated lines) supply rhythm and meaning in a story, poem, or song.

RL.3.4. Determine the meaning of words and phrases as they are used in a text, distinguishing literal from nonliteral language.

RL.4.4. Determine the meaning of words and phrases as they are used in a text, including those that allude to significant characters found in mythology (e.g., Herculean).

RL.5.4. Determine the meaning of words and phrases as they are used in a text, including figurative language such as metaphors and similes.

The following standards are found under Reading Informational Text:

RI.K.4. With prompting and support, ask and answer questions about unknown words in a text.

RI.1.4. Ask and answer questions to help determine or clarify the meaning of words and phrases in a text.

RI.2.4. Determine the meaning of words and phrases in a text relevant to a grade 2 topic or subject area.

RI.3.4. Determine the meaning of general academic and domain-specific words and phrases in a text relevant to a grade 3 topic or subject area.

RI.4.4. Determine the meaning of general academic and domain-specific words or phrases in a text relevant to a grade 4 topic or subject area.

RI.5.4. Determine the meaning of general academic and domain-specific words and phrases in a text relevant to a grade 5 topic or subject area.

Tier 1 words are generally not a problem for most students; however, English language learners will have to be watched carefully. Tier 1 words are words that most students know, and many, perhaps most, of these words are acquired through conversation and without considerable effort. Tier 1 words are not included in the CCSS.

Tier 2 words are usually gleaned from text as opposed to conversation. These words appear across the curriculum and are useful in both writing and reading. They often denote indirect or specific ways to convey information. A Tier 2 word would be *stroll* to replace the more common word *walk*. These words require purposeful teaching.

Tier 3 words are specific to a domain or field of study and must be learned in order for students to understand new ideas, concepts, and facts. We find Tier 3 words more often in informational text, but they are not limited to any specific genre. These are often words with which students have difficulty, and many texts define them in context, repeat them, and make them part of a lexicon, if one is included. Most teachers teach these words explicitly, before the students read the text. The use of one of the vocabulary word maps in the appendix of this book may be helpful for teaching Tier 3 words.

General Academic Words

Some of our students are literally literacy impoverished. They come from backgrounds in which there was minimal or no reading aloud by a primary caregiver and few, if any, books or reading materials in the home. The beauty of general academic words is that they can be taught indirectly. Reading aloud to your students from a varied selection of texts and genres will improve their vocabularies as long as the texts you use are at and above grade level.

Few or Flood?

Michael Pressley stated at the 2006 International Reading Association's Reading Research Conference, "In settings where literacy achievement is going well, teachers flood the classroom with vocabulary and vocabulary instruction" (p. 14), an approach that "would contrast considerably with some of the vocabulary instruction currently proposed as deserving more attention in classrooms—for example, the in-depth teaching of a relatively few words" (p. 15). This does not mean that teachers don't choose Tier 2 words for direct instruction; this is in addition to the "flooding" of words.

Pressley said that teachers should be using *interactive read-alouds*, independent and teacher-directed readings so that students can experience dozens of new words each day, wall charts that students can use to see multiple meanings of words that students are expected to use in writing and know on tests, and lessons in every subject area that are filled with vocabulary.

Pressley's suggestions have been studied with some impressive results. The study done by Labbo, Love, and Ryan (2007) was an electronically enhanced vocabulary flood. Students were given Pressley's suggestions, and some digital work was also added. It yielded pre-to-posttest increases in percentages of students at or above average that went from 13 percent to 39 percent on receptive and 24 percent to 57 percent on expressive vocabulary measures. These impressive results were from kindergarten through 2nd grade.

Baumann, Ware, and Edwards (2007) released a cascade of vocabulary in a 5th-grade classroom over a full school year. The researchers found that students used 36 percent more total words and 42 percent more low-frequency words in writing samples at the end of the program than they did at the beginning. Their expressive vocabulary acquisition exceeded expectations for the school year. Students with below-average receptive vocabularies at the beginning of the year made greater gains than students who started the year with above-average word knowledge. What is also important to note is that students changed their attitudes toward vocabulary learning.

In another study Biemiller (2004) concluded that "children with initially smaller vocabularies (specific to the books instructed) have at least the same gains and sometimes even larger gains" than word-wiser peers and that "those with relatively smaller vocabularies are most in need of added words" (p. 37). Research has shown us that students who enter school with fewer vocabulary words fall behind their peers (Hart & Risley, 1995).

Domain Specific

Because domain-specific words are unfamiliar and important for the understanding of the topic, teachers are more likely to choose these words to define. They are usually presented explicitly and then used repeatedly while covering the topic. These words are often found in bold type or italics and they are defined within the text. If there is a glossary, these words are usually found there. This is an important point because the definition in the glossary is going to be the correct definition for the word as it is found in context.

Example Grade 4–5 Text Complexity Band from Appendices A and B

Italics = *Tier 2*, <u>Underlined</u> = Tier 3

> In *early times*, no one knew how <u>volcanoes</u> formed or why they *spouted red-hot* <u>molten</u> rock. In *modern times*, scientists began to study <u>volcanoes</u>. They still don't know all the answers, but they know much about how a <u>volcano</u> works. Our planet is made up of many *layers* of rock. The top *layers* of *solid* rock are called the <u>crust</u>. Deep beneath the crust is the <u>mantle</u>, where it is so hot that some rock melts. The melted, or <u>molten</u>, rock is called <u>magma</u>.
>
> <u>Volcanoes</u> are *formed* when <u>magma</u> pushes its way up through the crack in Earth's crust. This is called a <u>volcanic</u> *eruption*. When <u>magma</u> *pours forth* on the *surface,* it is called <u>lava</u>.
>
> Simon, Seymour. *Volcanoes*. New York: HarperCollins, 2006.

Would you have chosen the same words for Tier 2 and Tier 3? Sometimes it is not easy to decide which words are Tier 2 and not Tier 1 because we know the definition, it seems common to us, and we assume that others know it. Perhaps we have even taught a particular Tier 2 word and expected our students to recognize it in any context and understand it.

So Many Words; So Little Time

How does one select the right words to be taught explicitly? We must ask ourselves a few questions:

- How important is the word to the text now being studied?
- How useful is this word across the curriculum?
- Does the word assist students in making connections to prior knowledge and personal experiences?

If you are in a self-contained classroom and teach all of the subjects, you will have a grasp of what words are taught across the content areas. Marzano and Pickering (2005) suggest that you consider how many words you will teach in a week. Three? Five? Ten? How many will be Tier 2 words and how many will be Tier 3?

By teaching the critical verbs and nouns in this text, you will be teaching 50 or more Tier 2 words. As you look at your textbooks and supplemental reading materials, you will see how many of the critical words are necessary for your students to know. If you use the pre-assessment, you may have a better idea of what words you don't have to teach explicitly.

If you also use the "flooding" method described earlier, it appears you will be enriching your students' vocabulary exponentially. Discuss this information with your colleagues, administrators, or district. Some districts have developed their own lists of words. As a district or school you may decide to create your lists now. Marzano and Pickering (2005) suggest these phases or stages of development

1. Decide on the number of words to be taught at each grade level and in each content area.
2. Create a rank-ordered list of words for each academic content area.

3. Based on the length of these lists, figure out how many words should be taught in each academic area.
4. Create the final list after making additions and deletions.
5. Assign the terms to specific grades.

There are several lists available in *Vocabulary Games for the Classroom* (Carleton & Marzano, 2010).

Tiers Without Tears

If you are on your own as far as word selection, here is an idea from some teachers in Illinois.

Instead of going through your text before the students begin to read it, picking out all of the Tier 2 and Tier 3 words you think they don't know, share the process with your students.

Ask students to read the first chapter or supplemental materials for the topic. If you are teaching English/language arts, it may be a novel that you are teaching. Have the students make lists of the words they don't know. Explain to them that they are going to be helping not only their class but future classes as well, and you want them to do an exemplary job. (Use *exemplary* and add to their vocabulary.) Make them feel important.

You may want them to make a list on a three-column chart. The first column would have the words. The second column would read "Not Sure." The third column would be "Definitely Don't Know." Some teachers have students write down all interesting or unusual words even if they know them, adding a fourth column with the heading "I Know This One!"

The teachers found that by using this process they got a better feel for what the students needed to work on. Assure them that they aren't going to have to write these words in a notebook, look them up in a dictionary, and then refer back to the text. Tell them that learning vocabulary will be fun, and convince them that this will make a difference to them, as well as to future classes.

Compile the lists or charts. Choose the least known words that you feel are important and worthwhile to take the time to teach explicitly. Check that list over carefully and determine whether you are dealing with more Tier 2 or

Tier 3 words. Your classes are probably very diverse, and you will have students who are light-years ahead of others in vocabulary. They don't have to be involved in the explicit instruction of the words they know. There will be those students who have very long lists or who won't make the lists because the process is too painful—all the words seem difficult to them. It's time to differentiate your instruction.

Starting a Deluge

The flooding strategy appears to be a sound one. How do you do it? According to Brabham et al. (2012), there are three things that need to be done: word integration, repetition, and meaningful use.

Integration can be accomplished by using gestalts (Nilsen & Nilsen, 2005, p. 200) and clustering words. This teaching word means relationships among known words and many new words at the same time. Marzano (1984) suggested that effective vocabulary programs should take advantage of gestalts and semantic clusters that make up language to provide "necessary associations of new words to old words and conceivably escalate the rate at which students learn new items" (p. 173). Studies show that when words were taught in meaning-based gestalts or clusters, word knowledge and comprehension improved significantly. This was true for English language learners as well as students who were native English speakers (Durso & Coggins, 1991).

Repetition of word relationships can be accomplished by creating text sets that fall into the same category and grade level. A text set for kindergarten through upper elementary with the concept of "Feelings" might look like this:

Cain, J. (2000). *The way I feel*. New York: Scholastic.
Coles, R. (1995). *The story of Ruby Bridges*. New York: Scholastic.
Janovitz, M. (1994). *Look out, bird!* New York: North-South.
Lindbergh, R. (1990). *The day the goose got loose*. New York: Penguin.
Lionni, L. (1987). *Nicholas, where have you been?* New York: Knopf.
Penn, A. (1993). *The kissing hand*. Terre Haute, IN: Tanglewood.
Ringgold, F. (1999). *If a bus could talk: The story of Rosa Parks*. New York: Aladdin.
Steig, W. (1969). *Sylvester and the magic pebble*. New York: Aladdin.

Meaningful use comes from seeing or hearing the same word in multiple texts, discovering multiple meanings of words, making rhymes, finding words in context, and generally playing with words.

Interactive Read-Alouds

This is a powerful teaching tool that is backed by research and encourages all students to be involved in learning. Interactive read-alouds have the following components:

- Previewing the book
- Scaffolding on prior knowledge
- Modeling vocabulary development
- Teaching reading fluency
- Emphasizing elements of the story
- Asking purposeful questions
- Using think-alouds to assist comprehension
- Summarizing the story to bring closure

Previewing the book involves discussing the title, author, and genre. Look at the cover of the book and let students predict what the book will be about from the cover and the title. Ask students if there is an illustrator and discuss what that means. Check out the cover art and discuss what kind of illustration it is. Look at the back cover and read what has been written to try to hook the reader. You may wish to do a picture walk-through of the book for younger students or nonreaders.

Read the book aloud. Read slowly, but fluently. If you are the only person who reads aloud to them, it is very important that you model the fluency you want to hear from them as readers. Underline words with your voice. Simply by the way you read, students will be able to tell what words are important to know. You may stop occasionally to share what you are thinking, but don't interrupt the flow of the book too much.

Following the reading, ask questions. Avoid yes or no questions; dig deeper. "What was the character like? What evidence is there from the text that supports your answer? Let's revisit the text and find out."

Find out more about interactive read-alouds at http://www.primary-education-oasis.com/interactive-read-aloud.html#.UGruxk3pdLc

CHAPTER 7

Making Them Stick

Mastering these words will take the cooperation and encouragement of all staff members. Perhaps the pre-assessments provided in Chapters 3 and 4 will be helpful. If all teachers give the pre-assessment, your staff can see how you stand in relation to these words that are so important for the standards and college and career readiness. If you teach in a high-poverty school or you have a large population of English language learners, you may find that these words are not part of the vocabularies of the majority of your students. If that is the case, several suggestions in this chapter may help you.

Classroom Strategies

1. All of the activities and templates provided can be used for any of the words. As you try activities and find them successful, use them with other words as well. Just remember that novelty can wear off quickly, so spread out the use of some of those strategies as you see your students becoming bored.
2. Make one of the words the "Word of the Week" in all classrooms/ content areas of your grade level. This will get everyone involved with the

words. Hang a poster of the word in the cafeteria, library, hallway, and even in the bathrooms.

3. Music, art, and physical education teachers can be a big part of this process.

    • Music teachers: help the students write a song for the critical verbs.
    • Art teachers: help with the posters or even more creative projects to help students remember.
    • P.E. teachers: movement is so important for many of our learners. Could they jump rope as they are reciting jingles? Could you use the word *demonstrate* and *develop* in your directions or dialogue with students?

4. Be certain to use the words in any tests and quizzes that you give.

5. Students need to see the words on a regular basis. If we want the words to get into long-term memory, they need plenty of repetition.

6. Get students involved in creating assessments. As they do, give them a minimum number of the critical words that they must include on the assessment. This will provide several challenges: knowing what the critical words mean, how they can be used, and what the content that they are studying is really about.

7. Vocabulary word maps, concept maps, mind maps, or other graphic organizers should be used with almost every word. Give students the opportunity to put the word in a spot that can be remembered as a picture.

8. After you and the class have decided on a simple definition, start working on the jingle. You may write your own jingle if your definition and the jingle in this book do not match. Also, know that a jingle, song, or rap that the students make up themselves will have emotional connections for them and therefore be more meaningful and memorable. Do whatever it takes to get the word into long-term memory. Students may want to make up movements for the word and definition. That will enhance memory by adding the kinesthetic component.

9. Popular songs have great melodies that students know. I always had my students put prepositions, helping verbs, and other terms to music. They

chose their own song and sang the words to that song. With the critical words, they could choose one word or several and sing the word, definition, and some sentences to the music. Students could work in groups and you could have some friendly competition. Better yet, divide those critical words up among the groups. Each group creates a song and then teaches the rest of the class their song. All of the words studied thus far would be set to music, and all the students would know them.

10. Have students visit other classes and share their songs or raps with them. Because all students need to know these words, this would provide more repetition, be a lot of fun, and give the various grade levels some common ground. Great relationship building!

11. Take nursery rhymes, favorite poems, or quotes and have students rewrite them using the critical words.

> Mary had a little lamb,
>
> she analyzed her well.
>
> Her point of view became brand new,
>
> as she found she could not spell!

12. Practice the jingle several times the first day and daily after that. As students line up for different activities, have them recite the jingles. Try using some of the activities that you like for the word.

13. When you start the next word, be certain you spiral back and review previous words.

14. Use a review activity after the number of words you feel is appropriate for your grade level. I have them spaced out about every seven words.

15. Teach one word at a time. *Compare* and *contrast* and *summarize* and *paraphrase* are the only verbs I suggest you might teach together. Some teachers don't teach them at the same time, and some don't even teach them consecutively. *Metaphor* and *simile* and *tone* and *mood* are also taught together.

16. Some words need to be taught in succession, because it just makes sense. For instance, *central idea/main idea*, *details*, *support*, and *evidence* could be taught sequentially. I have them listed in the book alphabetically, so they are easier to find.

17. Understanding these words, their definitions, and how to use them or draw them will take time. Remember that if your whole school follows the plan with these words, each year it will be easier to teach the words of the standards. Although new words are added most years, by 5th grade the bulk of the words will be known.

Of course you have other vocabulary to teach, but remember the importance of these words because they appear on assessments.

Schoolwide Strategies

Back to School Night: A Critical Celebration

Parental support of the critical words will be helpful. Why not have the classrooms, the auditorium, and the cafeteria filled with posters of the words? This shows parents and caregivers that these words are important to their children. Hand out a list of the words at the open house and discuss how everyone at school will be modeling the use of the words. Explain that one thing they can do to help their children is to use the words at home.

Weekly or Monthly Newsletter

Send the "Word of the Week" home with its definition, the jingle, and sample sentences that could be used at home by the parents. Ask parents to quiz their children on the word of the week or any previous words that have been sent home in the letter.

The Academic Pep Assembly

Cheerleaders love to cheer . . . about anything! Why not have the occasional Pep Assembly to get students excited about learning the words they need to know for the standards and for life. When I was a cheerleading coach, we often had pep assemblies before our standardized testing. It showed the students that the test was important and offered them test-taking tips in the form of cheers. Many students repeated the cheers before they took the test.

Websites

Put the critical word of the week on the school website along with the definition and some sentences. Individual classrooms that have websites can do the same. Perhaps if every class has its own website, it could share how well the class is doing with the critical words.

The Critical Talent Show

Have classrooms or groups of students sign up to sing their own personal song or one of the jingles with movements or dance steps that go with the word. This will give other classes ideas and perhaps trigger a memory for the word or words that they need help to remember. (Wasn't it funny that Johnny did two backflips when his class sang the song to *compare* and *contrast*? James tried to do backflips at the same time, but he did a forward flip instead! I'll never forget the difference between those words again!)

Community Strategies

Get the Community Involved

If your school has a community partner, ask them to participate. They can send over employees to talk about how the critical words are part of their jobs. They can also put up posters of the words in their place of business. Ask other businesses to participate, too. The stores that students and parents frequent may be very willing to join in the learning and the fun! Community leaders and local government officials may be willing to talk to the students about how these words are part of their work vocabulary.

Guest Speakers

Parents, community members, teachers, and other faculty members may be willing and able to speak to the words. For example, the cafeteria staff has to "organize" the food and "distinguish" between the types of nutritional components for breakfast and lunch.

Preschool

Public and private preschools and daycares also need to have this information. See if they are willing to begin using some of the critical vocabulary at their locations. Perhaps your school can provide posters for them. Some of the classes may be able to visit the preschools and sing the jingles, songs, or raps.

So What? Now What?

Where do you want to begin? If you are more comfortable starting small, pick a word and focus on your own class. See how quickly and easily it goes. Use activities from any section of the book that you feel will work well for your students.

If you want to start big, particularly if you are the librarian, principal, assistant principal, or someone else who can start a critical word movement, look at the suggestions in this chapter and get started. It's never too late, and it's never too soon to get our students' vocabularies growing!

Appendix: Templates

Vocabulary Gloves
Frayer Model
Venn Diagram
Synonym Wheel
Vocabulary Word Map
Vocabulary Word Map
Comparison/Contrast Organizer
Cube Template

Vocabulary Gloves

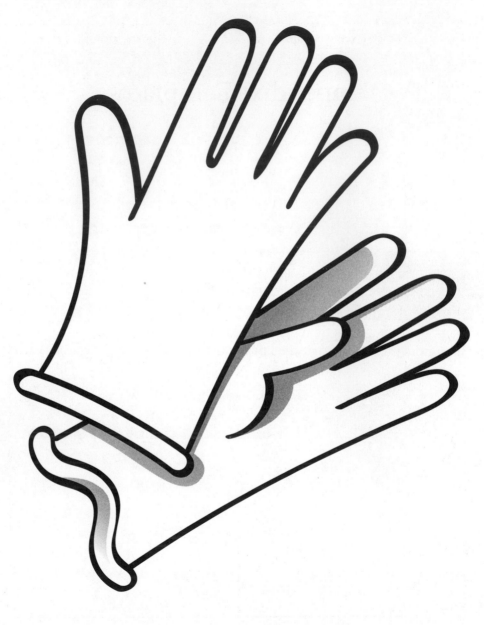

Frayer Model

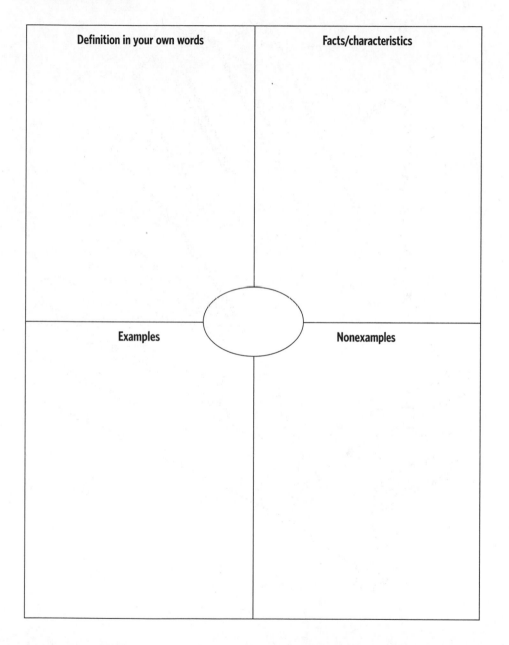

Venn Diagram

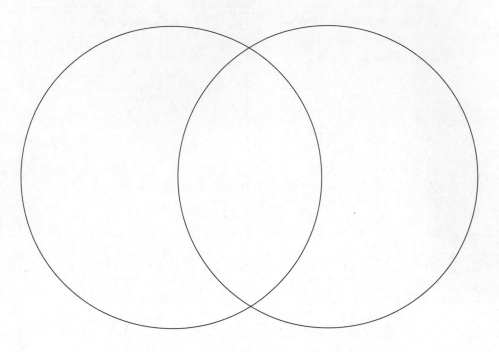

Concept Map

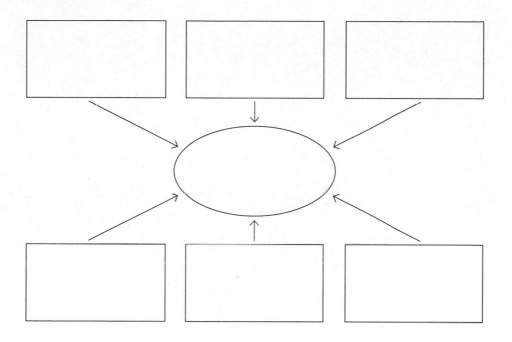

Synonym Wheel

Vocabulary Word Map

Write the word.

Write a definition of
the word.

Write a synonym.

Write an antonym.

Write the word here, in color.

Use the word in a sentence
that shows its meaning.

Draw a picture showing the
meaning of the word.

Vocabulary Word Map

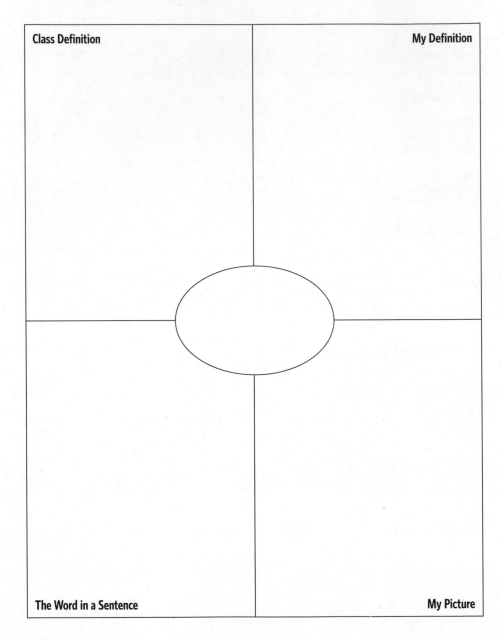

Comparison/Contrast Organizer

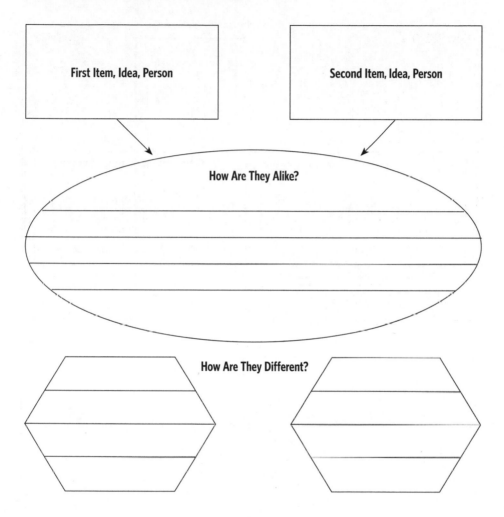

First Item, Idea, Person

Second Item, Idea, Person

How Are They Alike?

How Are They Different?

Cube Template

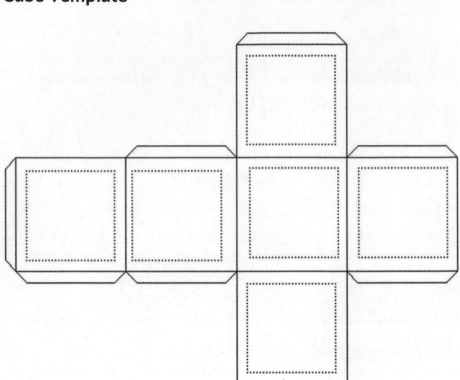

References

Anderson, L. W., & Krathwohl, D. R. (Eds.). (2001). *A taxonomy for learning, teaching, and assessing: A revision of Bloom's taxonomy of educational objectives: Complete edition.* New York: Longman.

Ash, P., Benedek, E., & Scott, C. (1999). *Principles and practice of child and adolescent forensic psychiatry.* Washington, DC: American Psychiatric Publishing.

Baker, S., Simmons, D., & Kame'enui, E. (1997). Vocabulary acquisition: Research bases. In D. Simmons & E. Kame'enui (Eds.), *What reading research tells us about children with diverse learning needs: Bases and basics.* Mahwah, NJ: Erlbaum.

Baumann, J., Ware, D., & Edwards, E. (2007). "Bumping into spicy, tasty words that catch your tongue": A formative experiment on vocabulary instruction. *The Reading Teacher, 61*(2), 108–122.

Beck, I. L., McKeown, M. G., & Kucan, L. (2002). *Bringing words to life.* New York: Guilford.

Bellanca, P. (1998). *Ending the essay.* Writing Center at Harvard University. Retrieved September 27, 2012, from http://www.fas.harvard.edu/~wricntr/documents/Conclusions.html

Biemiller, A. (2004). Teaching vocabulary in the primary grades: Vocabulary instruction needed. In J. Bauman & E. Kame'enui (Eds.), *Vocabulary instruction: Research to practice* (pp. 28–40). New York: Guilford.

Bloom, B. S. (Ed.). 1956. *Taxonomy of educational objectives: The classification of educational goals: Handbook I, cognitive domain.* New York: Longman.

Brabham, E., Buskist, C., Henderson, S. C., Paleologos, T., & Baugh, N. (2012). Flooding vocabulary gaps to accelerate word learning. *The Reading Teacher, 55*(8), 523–533.

Bronson, P., & Merryman, A. (2009). *Nurture shock: New thinking about children.* New York: Twelve, Hatchett Book Group.

Carleton, L., & Marzano, R. (2010). *Vocabulary games for the classroom.* Bloomington, IN: Marzano Research Laboratory.

Coleman, D. (2011, April 28). *Bringing the Common Core to life*. Presentation made in Albany, NY. Retrieved from New York State Education Department at http://usny.nysed.gov/rttt/docs/bringingthecommoncoretolife/part6transcript.pdf

D'Antoni A. V., Zipp, G. P., & Olson, V. G. (2009). Interrater reliability of the mind map assessment rubric in a cohort of medical students. *BMC Medical Education, 9*, 19.

Dean, C. B., Hubbell, E. R., Pitler, H., & Stone, B. (2012). *Classroom instruction that works: Research-based strategies for increasing student achievement* (2nd ed.). Alexandria, VA: ASCD.

DeTemple, J., & Tabors, P. O. (1996). *Children's story retelling as a predictor of early reading achievement.* ERIC Document Reproduction Service No. ED 403 543.

Doidge, N. (2007). *The brain that changes itself.* New York: Penguin Books.

Durso, F. T., & Coggins, K. A. (1991). Organized instruction for the improvement of word knowledge skills. *Journal of Educational Psychology, 83*, 108–112.

Dye, G. A. (2000). Graphic organizers to the rescue! Helping students link—and remember—information. *Teaching Exceptional Children, 32*(3), 72–76.

Elster, C., & Simons, H. (1985). How important are illustrations in children's readers? *The Reading Teacher, 39*(2), 148–152.

Farah, M. J., Noble, K. G., Hurt, H. (2005) Poverty, privilege, and brain development: Empirical findings and ethical implications. In J. Illes (Ed.), *Neuroethics: Defining the issues in theory, practice, and policy*. New York: Oxford University Press.

Farah, M. J., Savage, J., Brodsky, N. L., Shera, D., Malamud, E., Giannetta, J., & Hurt, H. (2004). Association of socioeconomic status with neurocognitive development. *Pediatric Research* (Suppl.).

Fisher, D., Frey, N., & Lapp, D. (2009). *In a reading state of mind*. Newark, DE: International Reading Association.

Fisher, D., Zike, D., & Frey, N. (2007, August). Foldables: Improving learning with 3-D interactive graphic organizers. *Classroom Notes Plus,* 1–12.

Frayer, D., Frederick, W. C., & Klausmeier, H. J. (1969). *A schema for testing the level of cognitive mastery*. Madison: Wisconsin Center for Education Research.

Gazzaniga, M. (Organizer), & C. Asbury & B. Rich (Eds.) (2008). *Learning, arts, and the brain: The Dana Consortium report on arts and cognition* (pp. 11–16). New York: Dana Press.

Gelb, M. (1995). *Mind mapping*. New York: Nightingale-Conant.

Hackman, D., & Farah, M. (2009). Socioeconomic status and the developing brain. *Trends in Cognitive Sciences, 13*(2), 65–73.

Harris, J. (2006). *No two alike*. New York: W.H. Horton

Hart, B., & Risley, T. (1995). *Meaningful differences in the everyday experiences of young American children*. Baltimore: Paul Brookes.

Jensen, E. (2009). *Teaching with poverty in mind: What being poor does to kids' brains and what schools can do about it*. Alexandria, VA: ASCD.

Jonides, J. (2008). Musical skill and cognition. In M. Gazzaniga (Organizer) & C. Asbury & B. Rich (Eds.), *Learning, arts, and the brain: The Dana Consortium report on arts and cognition* (pp. 11–16). New York: Dana Press.

Kaye, P. (1984). *Games for reading.* New York: Pantheon.

Koutstaal, W., Buckner, R. L., Schacter, D. L., & Rosen, B. R. (1997, March). An fMRI study of item repetition during an auditorily cued word generation task. *Abstracts of the Cognitive Neuroscience Society,* Boston, p. 68.

Klingberg, T., Fernell, E., Olesen, P. J., Johnson, M., Gustafsson, P., Dahlstrom, K., et al. (2005). Computerized training of working memory in children with ADHD: A randomized, controlled trial. *Journal of the American Academy of Child and Adolescent Psychiatry, 44,* 177–186.

Labbo, L. D., Love, M. S., & Ryan, T. (2007). A vocabulary flood: Making words "sticky" with computer-response activities. *The Reading Teacher, 60*(6), 582–588. doi:10.1598/RT.60.6.10.

Marzano, R. J. (1984). A cluster approach to vocabulary instruction: A new direction from the research literature. *The Reading Teacher, 38*(2), 168–173.

Marzano, R. J. (2004). *Building background knowledge for academic achievement: Research on what works in schools.* Alexandria, VA: ASCD.

Marzano, R., & Pickering, D. (2005). *Building academic vocabulary: Teacher's manual.* Alexandria, VA: ASCD.

Marzano, R., Pickering, D., & Pollack, J. (2001). *Classroom instruction that works.* Alexandria, VA: ASCD.

Medina, J. (2008). *Brain rules.* Seattle, WA: Pear Press.

Nagy, W. E., & Anderson, R. C. (1984). How many words are there in printed school English? *Reading Research Quarterly, 19,* 304–330.

National Governors Association Center for Best Practices, Council of Chief State School Officers. (2010). *Common Core State Standards for Reading.* Washington, DC: Authors.

Nilsen, A., & Nilsen, D. (2005). Vocabulary development: Teaching vs. testing. In R. Robinson (Ed.), *Readings in reading instruction* (pp. 196–204). New York: Pearson.

Payne, R. (2009). *A framework for understanding poverty.* Highlands, TX: Aha! Process.

Pearson, P. D., & Gallagher, G. (1983). The gradual release of responsibility model of instruction. *Contemporary Educational Psychology, 8,* 112–123.

Pereira, A. C., Huddleston, D. E., Brickman, A. M., Sosunov, A. A., Hen, R., McKhann, G. M., Sloan, R., et al. (2007). An in vivo correlate of exercise-induced neurogenesis in the adult dentate gyrus. *Proceedings of the National Academy of Sciences of the United States of America, 104*(13), 5638–5643.

Perry, B. D. (2001). The neurodevelopmental impact of violence in childhood. In D. Schetky & E. P. Benedek (Eds.), *Textbook of child and adolescent rorensic psychiatry* (pp. 221–238). Washington, DC: American Psychiatric Press.

Phillips, V., & Wong, C. (2012, April 6). *Teaching to the common core by design not accident.* Phi Delta Kappa International. Available http://www.edweek.org/ew/articles/2012/04/01/kappan_phillips.html

Piaget, J. (1970). *Genetic epistemology.* (E. Duckworth, Trans.). New York: Columbia University Press.

Powell, R. R., & Pohndorf, R. H. (1971). Comparison of adult exercisers and nonexercisers on fluid intelligence and selected physiological variables. *Research Quarterly, 42*(1), 70–77.

Pressley, M. (2006, April 29). *What the future of reading research could be.* Paper presented at the International Reading Association's Reading Research Conference 2006, Chicago. Retrieved October 1, 2012, from www.reading.org/downloads/publications/videos/rrc-06-pressley_paper.pdf

RAND Reading Study Group. (2002). *Reading for understanding: Toward a research and development program in reading comprehension.* Santa Monica, CA: Office of Education Research and Improvement.

Ratey, J. (2008). *Spark.* New York: Little, Brown, & Company.

Schacter, D. L. (2001). *The seven sins of memory: How the mind forgets and remembers.* Boston: Houghton Mifflin.

Silver, H. Dewing, R. & Perini, M. (2012). *The Core Six: Essential strategies for achieving excellence with the Common Core.* Alexandria, VA: ASCD.

Snowdon, D. (2001). *Aging with grace.* New York: Bantam Books.

Sprenger, M. (2005). *How to teach so students remember.* Alexandria, VA: ASCD.

Sprenger, M. (2010). *Brain-based teaching in the digital age.* Alexandria, VA: ASCD.

Squire, L., & Kandel, E. (2000). *Memory: From mind to molecules.* New York: Scientific American Library.

Tileston, D. (2011, February). Motivating students. Paper presented at the Learning and the Brain Conference, San Francisco, CA.

Tileston, D. & Darling, S. (2008). *Why culture counts: Teaching children of poverty.* Bloomington, IN: Solution Tree.

Webb, N. L. (2005). *Alignment, depth of knowledge, and change.* Madison: Wisconsin Center for Education Research.

Willis, J. (2006). *Researched-Based Strategies to Ignite Student Learning.* Alexandria, VA: ASCD.

Worcester, T. (2010). *50 Quick & Easy Computer Activities for Kids.* Eugene, OR: Visions Technology in Education

Wormeli, R. (2005). *Summarization in any subject: 50 techniques to improve student learning.* Alexandria, VA: ASCD.

Zike, D. (1992). *Big book of books.* San Antonio: Dinah-Might Adventures.

About the Author

 **Marilee Sprenger** is a highly regarded educator, presenter, and author who has taught students from pre-kindergarten through graduate school. She has been translating neuroscience research for more than 20 years and has engaged audiences internationally. The author of eight books and numerous articles, Marilee is a popular keynote speaker who is passionate about brain-research-based teaching strategies, which include differentiated instruction and wiring the brain for success.

Marilee is a member of the American Academy of Neurology, the Learning and the Brain Society, and the Cognitive Neuroscience Society. She is an adjunct professor at Aurora University, teaching graduate courses on brain-based teaching, learning and memory, and differentiation. Teachers who have read Marilee's work or heard her speak agree that they walk away with user-friendly information that can be applied at all levels.

You can contact Marilee at brainlady@gmail.com or visit her website brainlady.com.

Related ASCD Resources: Vocabulary of the Common Core

At the time of publication, the following ASCD resources were available (ASCD stock numbers appear in parentheses). For up-to-date information about ASCD resources, go to www.ascd.org. You can search the complete archives of *Educational Leadership* at http://www.ascd.org/el.

ASCD EDge Group

Exchange ideas and connect with other educators interested in teaching the vocabulary of the Common Core on the social networking site ASCD EDge™ at http://ascdedge.ascd.org/

Online Courses

English Language Learners and the Common Core State Standards (#PD13OC002)
Common Core and Literacy Strategies: English Language Arts (#PD11OC135)
Common Core and Literacy Strategies: History/Social Studies (#PD11OC132)
Common Core and Literacy Strategies: Mathematics (#PD11OC134)
Common Core and Literacy Strategies: Science (#PD11OC133)

Print Products

Brain-Based Teaching in the Digital Age by Marilee Sprenger (#110018)
Common Core Standards for Middle School English Language Arts: A Quick-Start Guide by Susan Ryan and Dana Frazee; edited by John Kendall (#113012)
Common Core Standards for High School English Language Arts: A Quick-Start Guide by Susan Ryan and Dana Frazee; edited by John Kendall (#113010)
How to Teach So Students Remember by Marilee Sprenger (#105016)
Learning and Memory: The Brain in Action by Marilee Sprenger (#199213)
Teaching Basic and Advanced Vocabulary: A Framework for Direct Instruction by Robert J. Marzano (#309113)
Teaching Vocabulary Across the Content Areas: An ASCD Action Tool by Camille Blachowicz and Charlene Cobb (#707035)

The Whole Child Initiative helps schools and communities create learning environments that allow students to be healthy, safe, engaged, supported, and challenged. To learn more about other books and resources that relate to the whole child, visit www.wholechildeducation.org.

For more information: send e-mail to member@ascd.org; call 1-800-933-2723 or 703-578-9600, press 2; send a fax to 703-575-5400; or write to Information Services, ASCD, 1703 N. Beauregard St., Alexandria, VA 22311-1714 USA.